Hillard –
Thank you for
being such a joy to
Marry and for giving
our story a chance.
Well wishes,
Katie B

BROKEN
NEK

Hillard –
You are such a
joy to chat with each
week. I'm glad I got to meet
& know you. Thank you for
your int[erest] in our
story.

A MEMOIR
BY KATIE ALBRECHT
AND MARY ALBRECHT

BROKEN NEK

FINDING
THE FAMILY
YOU NEVER KNEW
YOU ALWAYS
WANTED

gatekeeper press

Columbus, Ohio

Broken Nek: Finding the family you never knew you always wanted

Published by Gatekeeper Press
2167 Stringtown Rd, Suite 109
Columbus, OH 43123-2989
www.GatekeeperPress.com

ISBN (hardcover): 9781642373967
ISBN (paperback): 9781642373950
eISBN: 9781642373943

Printed in the United States of America

28 YEARS AGO

This is bad.

I am completely lost.

Driving alone as a 22-year-old female through the mountains of Virginia at dusk with minimal gasoline is beyond frightening. It dawns on me that I have no idea what happened between this moment and when I left the hotel in Ohio. I don't remember what route I took or any sights along the way. All I recall is the tears—gut wrenching sobs the entire drive— like an exorcism of pain and suffering coming out.

Is it possible to get so tired of something that your entire body burns from the inside out? I am repulsed by my family's twisted tolerance. I had to get out of there or else surely would have died from the cover-ups. Or am I overreacting like my mom always says? My thoughts are spinning, just as this road seems to be doing. Where the hell am I? I slap my cheeks in an effort to focus as haunting memories cloud my sense of direction.

Why didn't anyone ever believe me? How did I end up in the mental hospital when it should have been him? Why am I considered the problem child in the family?

Looking out the window now, I slow down for what seems like the hundredth dangerous curve and realize there will soon be blackness to either side of me. The only light belongs to my headlights and who knows if I will run out of road and plummet somewhere undiscoverable.

"Shit, shit, shit. How could I be so stupid?" I scream out loud, pounding the steering wheel with both palms. Adrenaline roars through my body as I think about the possibilities of what could happen if I don't get out of here tonight. I imagine bears attacking my car trying to maul me if I were to get stranded. I envision someone coming along and helping themselves to my limited assets—or to something worse. I fear that I will never find my way back, starving and slowly dying alone. Is this any better than what I left?

Winding cautiously through the dark and narrow mountain roads, a light appears in the distance. I squint to see a small building labeled 'General Store' and an ounce of relief bubbles within at finally finding civilization. The crunching of the gravel under my tires feels safely familiar as I pull into the parking lot and brake. My first sight of humanity since getting lost is of three men sitting to the side of the store's front door, enjoying some beers and cigarettes. They are laughing and bantering with each other, clearly enjoying just hanging out. The empty cans and dirty butts scattered on the ground indicate that they have been in this same place for quite a while. Despite my fatigue I cannot help but smile at the sweet sight of these old folks that remind me of my grandpa. Surely, they or someone else here can help me.

Continuing forward into an empty parking spot, I sandwich my car between two rusty pickup trucks that must belong to these men. My Honda Accord appears newer and better than ever in comparison. But as I catch the eyes of one of the 'grand-pas' darting toward my car, then to the trucks, then back to my car, my relief immediately morphs into uneasiness. The man says something to the others and they chuckle as they all look my way. Effortlessly lifting himself out of his chair, he glides across the lot toward my car while staring directly into my eyes. A bad feeling stabs at my stomach when I see that he is moving way too gracefully for an old man. I examine him again as he nears and realize that he is not old at all. None of them are. They are dirty. They are scary. They are drunk. But they are not old.

Suddenly I realize I stand out like a glowing target in this culture. This is not remotely like the straight-laced, crime-free community I have come from, and I am in way over my head. How could I let this happen? I have allowed the power of one human being to incite me to do something so out of character that I have even shocked myself. The emotions surrounding the *day I left have literally propelled me from suburban Midwest to the mountains of Virginia and I don't even remember driving here.*

Have I completely lost my mind?

Engine still running, I jam the car into reverse and kick up a cloud of dust. Back into the blackness I race. I turn on my wipers but my vision does not clear. Feverishly rubbing the windshield, I still cannot see. Pulling over, I realize that I'm sobbing again. It's not raining out at all. Plopping my head on the steering wheel, I close my swollen, aching eyes.

I know I need to find help. Yet all I can see is him. HIM. My older brother by two years and the nightmare of my childhood. My body shudders as I picture his menacing face.

The doctors said he was sick. They wanted to help. My mom said he was sick. She wanted us to leave him alone.

But why would you leave someone alone if they are sick? Especially if the illness IS their brain, then shouldn't mentally healthy people BE their brain? Otherwise the horror never ends.

Little did I know almost three decades later my niece, his daughter, would prove this to be true.

CHAPTER 1

KATIE:

It has been exactly one half hour since my father told me that I am no longer his daughter.

It was quick when it happened with no further arguments; he was on the way out with Mom to get his prescription at Walgreens. It wasn't the first time this happened, either. He has told me several variations of this and other insults growing up. We always encouraged each other not to listen to him, for he couldn't possibly mean it. He does this to everyone he is close to, like his own perverse way of showing his love. Each little insult, however, builds a new layer to the shaky foundation I call my family.

I let out a deep breath as I brush a loose strand of brown hair out of my face and continue to stare at the canvas of my ceiling, dark from the night enclosing around our house. My feet are restless, stirring and twitching as I wait for them to come home. My high school bedroom still looks the same as it did when growing up. From the drawings on the walls and 'Good Luck!' sport signs from friends, to the exact same pile of clothes and rubbish in the corner that neither I nor anyone else has bothered to organize since I moved out for college.

My mind directs itself to that old clothes pile and the potential of clearing it out, just like I have thought about doing since I came back here three weeks ago before Grandma died. But as the notion comes and goes like a bird outside the window, my body remains still on my bed. I reason with myself that they should be back soon, and I am already nervous about what that conversation will bring. I don't need to add the stress of cleaning my never-tamed room on top of it. Mom said we would talk about what happened tonight, and I want to get it over with as soon as possible. I hope this time we actually do it.

Dad has never been quite right. We used to blame it on the alcohol that he had a tendency to drink.

And drink…

…and drink.

His beers would come straight from Satan's refrigerator, bringing us all into our own pocket of Hell. My childhood, as a result, was a life of waiting. Waiting for the screaming to be over, waiting for him to pass out, waiting for the next night of terror to come around. Waiting was our playbook, but knowing when it would happen again was the game.

It took years for us to notice that beer wasn't the problem at all, but rather, an unpleasant side effect of mental illness. He went through his phases of sobriety, but our money would still mysteriously go missing from our wallets, and we endured daily no-win shouting matches no matter what. He went through days without a drop of alcohol; we went through the same days feeling incredible guilt—guilt that he would manipulate us into feeling. Alcohol hasn't touched his lips in the years since the accident; but opioids have been consumed in a plethora. It was one addiction transferred to another with the same scary person underneath it all.

'I was calling Walgreens!' Dad's furious denial still rings through my ears like the wails of an alarm clock in the early morning light. I especially angered him this time since I was the one who recorded his phone conversation. The *Walgreens* he spoke of must be his code word for his very own Pablo Escobar. I may be naïve when it comes to drug dealing, but I know people don't typically ask for *'Percs'* when they are calling a pharmacy.

I find myself doubting why I moved back here to my parents' house as a functional adult. College had just ended and Grandma's cancer was worsening at a speedy rate. The time I spent with her at the end of her life was important; however, I wonder if it was worth it. Did I really think Dad would change his ways if I suddenly moved back? I suppose I had hoped so, even knowing the chances were slim. I did, however, believe that I had grown up enough at the age of 22 to be able to deal with him in a better way. Mature and wise, now that I have a degree. I realize now that having a healthy relationship with him is a feat bordering on the realm of impossible. If history tells the future, I may never be strong enough to do that, especially considering every time I come back here, I am reminded why I have always wanted to leave.

A loud cranking noise sounds from the floor below, signaling the outside screen door opening. There are soft thuds, likely from someone pushing their hip into the second door to the house—the necessary force to get the damn thing to open. My head immediately turns toward the noise but I make no move to get up. I close my eyes as I brace myself for the long and intense confrontation ahead. I listen to their footsteps as they enter the kitchen, and the moving of furniture as they walk through the tight space. The more time we delay, the more likely it is for us to change our minds. Anxiety coils through my body at that thought and I finally sit up.

My sister, Sandra, is in her room, just two familiar steps across the hall from mine, but her door is closed and I hear she is on the phone. I choose not to bother her and instead maneuver my way through the hall that wraps tightly around the staircase in the other direction. The already narrow space is even more constricted with dressers lining the walls from years ago that we never got rid of. A sneeze escapes me, my nose tickled by the dust flying up from the top of the old furniture. When I free myself from the tangled mess and reach the stairwell, confusion surfaces as the scent of onions frying immediately hits me, recognizing that Mom must be cooking an untimely dinner.

This better not mean a ceasefire. We had our troops holding together earlier tonight: Sandra, Mom, and I talked Dad down for an hour after all of us heard the recordings of his drug deals. But he has yet to relent, to admit the truth. He may be a warrior, a terrifying one at that, but we are an army. He may win a lot of battles, but he hasn't yet won the war. We finally have proof of him calling a drug dealer; it has to be different this time. To reassure myself, I clench my phone in my hand, knowing that the recordings remain saved in it. I will refer back to them when he tries to alter our thoughts about him as he always does. We are ready for his game.

My feet slowly patter down the stairs towards the spicy aroma of the food cooking below. As I turn the corner to our kitchen, a wave of heat rushes to my body. Mom stands at the stove sautéing vegetables, the cluttered table just a mere foot or two away from her backside as it takes up almost the entire cramped kitchen.

"Hey, Mom. So what's going on?" I question her as I notice that Dad is not in the room. He must have made it to the couch in the living room around the corner. These days he doesn't spend much time elsewhere, typically lying in a pool of blankets and human grease from his lack of hygiene. It's gotten especially disgusting since the accident.

"I am making dinner," she responds simply, and I have to stop myself from rolling my eyes at her dense response. While my mother and I have gotten closer these past few weeks since I moved back in, I know that she doesn't always get me. Our wavelengths spread out in opposite directions and don't often connect.

Growing up, she never strayed from the stereotypical mother figure. The one who baked cookies for us, her three children, showing up to our sporting events with dozens of them to share with the team. 'That's my baby!' She used to cry out at Josh's football games whenever he did something even a little out of the ordinary, like a spin move to avoid a defender only to get tackled a few yards later. Josh, my older brother by five years, was always the favorite. He was the first born and only child until Sandra came along almost four years later, and me only 15 months after that.

There were also those times when things got scary around the house, even for our standards, and Mom would have us stay in a hotel or drive us around for a while until Dad passed out. She was strong in the sense of protecting us in the moment and somehow maintained a positive attitude throughout the torrential shit-storm.

"Okay, but couldn't you have done that after we talked?" I try to keep a calm voice.

"I don't know, probably." Mom continues to stir the food as I stare at her blankly. After all that has happened tonight, why does it feel so like I'm climbing uphill to get this conversation started?

"So… can't we talk first?" My voice has a hint of panic in it now.

"Well, he was pestering me so I'm just putting something together real quick," she replies simply.

"Let me get this straight." I pause, trying to wrap my head around my next question. "When he orders Percocet illegally for like the millionth time, you make him *dinner*?"

"No, I am making dinner for everyone," she responds with no elaboration.

"But everyone includes him?" I ask, already knowing the answer.

She hesitates before conjuring up her response, "Well, yeah, but I'm not happy about it."

Sirens blare loudly throughout my body like the moment before a tornado touches earth. The sound forces itself into every crevice as it loops around and around, filling me with dread in its wake. "I thought we were going to talk about the drug use. Now, it's like you are rewarding him."

"We will talk—later." Mom doesn't sound convincing.

Something clicks within me, like finding a missing puzzle piece and snapping it into place. "Why do I have a feeling that 'later' is your way of saying it's not going to happen?"

She huffs in response, "I'm not going to let him starve, Katie."

Her tone is fatigued and dismissive, as if saying '*End of discussion, Katie.*' I know that tone—I have used it on others. But why am I receiving it from her? I am not the one in the wrong here. Mom listened to the recordings of him ordering Percocet. She heard him scream terrible things at me, all of which I took a video of, but I am not supposed to react. She watched from behind while I stood between them so he wouldn't attack her to get the money in her purse. Yet somehow . . . somehow throughout all that, I am the problem. I'm a problem for wanting to stand up to him.

The sting of her betrayal has the strength of a thousand bees, a feeling that is both new and familiar to me being in this family. I don't think I can go through this cycle again. Our life has been a too-fast Ferris Wheel that never ends, with short on-top-of-the-world highs and devastatingly long-lasting lows. I am sick of the dizziness. I feel a tear rolling down my cheek as I speak again, my voice barely louder than a whisper.

"Oh my *God*." I turn on the spot, unable to look at her anymore, and make my way to the family room where I collapse into the recliner. My heart is racing; my head is spinning. Mom was a symbol of strength growing up and would get us out of the house when danger emerged. But she also blamed us for stirring the pot whenever Dad was simmering. So *was* she our strength? Or are we just grasping at anything we can to justify that our childhood was 'not that bad'? We didn't have the power to do anything, yet she did, often choosing not to use it. A heavy weight sits on my chest, a result of her rejection. Realization hits me hard that the ray of light I pictured her to be is now flickering out.

A couple of deep groans sound from the living room, signaling Dad getting up from the couch. There are a few heavy thuds from his feet hitting the floor before he turns the corner and into my line of vision. My body tenses as he faces his back to me and steps into the kitchen. He mutters something to Mom that I don't process due to the thick haze covering my consciousness. He then turns around and locks his eyes on me. He's still wearing the same flannel coat that he wore two hours before when the whole blow-up happened. His black gloves remain locked into place on his hands and his mangy navy blue beanie is pressed to the top of his head, matting some of his greasy front hairs to his forehead. It may be winter, but we are indoors and the heat stays at a steady 82 degrees. Since his frostbite accident, he is always cold. Similarly, so are his eyes. No warmth can be found there either.

"I just wanted to go to Walgreens, you should know that," he hisses at me, a bite in his words. "We just got my prescription!"

I close my eyes as a painful sob rattles me. He won. He *always* wins.

There have been many instances in my life when I have cried because of something Dad said, and it embarrasses me every single time it happens. I wish I could remain strong and get him to change his ways, but I never had the stamina to keep up with him. In fact, earlier tonight I depleted all my energy when his anger was at its height. I have always craved for him to want to comfort me when I am sad, especially when he is the reason behind it. Right now, I hope he could at least show me mercy, especially in light of Grandma's funeral just yesterday. Surely, he realizes that we are all hurting and he will show the humanity

I have always longed for. I have to believe it is in there somewhere.

"Yeah, you better cry." His attack tumbles out instead.

"Please leave me alone," I respond, my voice weak.

"Why would you want your father in pain? You are a despicable human being for wanting that." He is playing the victim again.

I shut my painfully swollen eyes in response and bring my hand to the bridge of my nose to apply pressure. I am not a *despicable human being* for doing what is right. Why does he always have to paint us into something we are not? I don't fight him this time though. I just want him to leave the room; my 'waiting for this to be over' game begins again.

He opens his mouth, clearly still angry and wanting to spew out more vile. Nothing really stops him, unless *he* wants to stop. I continue to cry, hoping that he'll just go away. Mom's head emerges from behind his shoulder and she looks at me, concerned. She tells him to leave me alone.

"Oh sure, gang up on me. Everyone's favorite pasttime!" he growls out to her in response.

"Just go, Ken," Mom says sharply, and gestures towards his 'bedroom,' formerly known as the living room. He scoffs again and throws his hands up in the air, but stomps off like a pouting child that's been sent to a timeout. I hear the creak of the old couch as his weight sinks down and he settles into his usual position. Mom goes back to the stovetop, not saying another word. Sharp pains shoot up my spine from the lack of lumbar support, and I lean back against the chair. I embrace the pain as a reminder that this nightmare is one that I cannot wake up from. I don't know where to go from here.

Footsteps sound from the top of the staircase moments later. Each of the individual steps have their own unique sound. Growing up, I memorized those sounds as a form of protection. Sandra and I would wait in our rooms after an argument erupted below, anxious for when those feet would hit the very top step and our turn would come.

I hear the final thud of the bottom stair, and the long, slender figure of Sandra emerges. I look up in her direction, a small amount of hope fluttering again. She gets it. She was my ally growing up. She has seen the darkest sides of this family, too, and knows how crazy this all is.

I try to make eye contact with her through my tear-stained vision, but she doesn't even glance at me as she turns the corner and disappears into the room where Dad is. When she was on the phone upstairs, it sounded like she was seeking advice. Maybe she will take the lead in stopping the drug deals. Maybe *she* can be the voice that helps Dad get clean. She heard the whole conversation too. '*Hurry, Katie,*' she said to me as I was fumbling with the recording device on my phone, the urgency in her voice signifying that the window to catch him in the act was quickly closing.

"Dad, can I talk to you for a sec?" she says to him with passion in her tone. Sandra has a flare for drama— even moving to Los Angeles a few years ago to pursue acting. But her reaction to this household dysfunction is beyond her drama. She gets wound up when Dad strikes the wrong nerve, even though she only sees him a couple of times a year. The image of her furiously screaming in his face earlier today cartwheels through my mind. She doesn't do that unless severely provoked. It's apparent just how much he brings the worst out in all of us. I wonder what her next approach will be.

"I came down to apologize to you," Sandra says calmly to him, and my mouth nearly hits the floor.

"What?" I whisper sharply to no one in particular. He grumbles his response while I try to close my frozen-in-place mouth, shock rumbling through my veins.

"I forgive you, Dad. Please, let me pray with you." There is a moment of silence between the two of them, the sound of fabric rubbing against carpet as my sister seems to shift herself onto the floor. She begins a prayer, but I tune it out, too wrapped up in the never-ending horror story that is us. Ever since she got re-baptized in her new church, prayer is her answer to everything. It's as if calling Dad out and forgiveness cannot coexist. And now, as they have this precious father-daughter bonding moment, I have never felt more alone.

I *am* alone.

"Are you alright?" Mom interrupts my thoughts as she enters the family room and puts a hand on my shoulder. "You look pretty upset."

"This isn't going to change, is it." What I say comes out more as a statement than a question. "The drugs, the abuse, the hatred from him—it is going to follow us around forever."

I want her to tell me I am wrong. I want her to yell, scream, and tell the world how brave she is and that she will not stand for this abuse anymore. I would be so proud and would back her up the entire way. I would defend her when times get hard with him. We could do it—all of us together—and would survive because we have each other to rely on. All she would have to do is say she is willing to put a stop to his behavior. I have to know that there is still a shot to fix this family.

The reality, however, is that I am met with silence. Thundering, boisterous silence.

The atmosphere shifts around us and a chill creeps its way up my spine. Despair wraps itself around my neck, choking me. I let out a sharp gasp as the dam breaks, unable to hold back the numerous emotions hitting me at once.

My breaths become staggered. Heat rushes to my tear-soaked face, and I feel like I am not getting enough oxygen. I take a deep breath, but it comes up short of what I need. The walls are closing in on me, while the air continues to thin. I am trapped. I stand up, thinking this will dissipate my panic. My feet teeter as I start to pace.

My body's reaction numbs my mind so much that, at first, I don't realize Sandra is standing in the doorway. I feel mortified as I try to catch my breath.

"Katie, you need to calm down. You are going to pass out if you don't." She sounds condescending. Surely, fainting would be better than this nightmare.

KATIE ALBRECHT AND MARY ALBRECHT

I glare at her through my swollen eyes as my anxiety attack begins to fade. She picks up my irritation.

"I'm in no way justifying what he did or how he spoke to you—-" Sandra tries to explain.

"But you are," I cut her off. "We are just going to let him win again and he learns nothing. He changes nothing."

Sandra doesn't respond, and for a moment I think I might be getting through to her. That is, until she looks me directly in the eye and I see the expression I never want from her, or from anyone.

Pity.

"We have to forgive him, Katie," she continues. I wish she would stop. "It will drive us insane if we don't." I see Mom nod in my peripheral vision.

I have watched a lot of horror movies that involve murder, torture, and manipulation. None of those films compare to the terror I feel in this moment. I am desperately trying to convince them to take action on something that has been destroying us—and destroying him—our entire lives. Why is this not more obvious to them? Why do their eyes pity me as if I'm the one who is messed up?

I exit the room to get away from their burning eyes. Climbing the stairs to my bedroom, I weigh my options. I know what I have to do; my sanity depends on it. Deep down I knew I shouldn't have moved back here in the first place. The fact that we have real, tangible proof of his wrongdoings—illegal wrongdoings—and he is still able to lie his way out of the consequences means there is something seriously wrong here. It is not a matter of *if* I leave anymore, it's a matter of *when*. As I plop onto my bed, a piece of paper slides out from under my comforter. I pick it up, recognizing my own handwriting:

> GOD GRANT ME THE SERENITY TO ACCEPT THE THINGS I CANNOT CHANGE, COURAGE TO CHANGE THE THINGS I CAN, AND WISDOM TO KNOW THE DIFFERENCE.

I copied down the 'Serenity Prayer' just a week ago, after Grandma died. She loved that prayer. I had been performing badly at work and was looking for anything to inspire me to be better. I do believe in God, but writing a prayer like that is as rare as an atheist attending church—I don't usually do it. This must be a sign.

I take a deep breath and the fog clears in my mind. I hastily grab my Pillow Pet and fleece-tie blanket off my bed. Rushing down the stairs, I scoop up my purse and sling my backpack over my shoulder, still packed from Grandma's funeral. Sandra is in the kitchen now, and she calls out to me as I run past.

"I'm not the enemy here, Katie."

I halt and glare at her again as I wonder what the hell she means by that. Does she think *I* am the enemy? I battle the ugly side of myself, the one that only comes out around that horrendous man in the other room, with thoughts of screaming at her until I can no longer speak. But I know if I do, then I will be like him. I cannot allow that.

"Neither am I," I defend myself, stoically. I continue and enter the family room once more to where Mom still sits.

"I can't stay here tonight," I say to her, *goodbye* thick in my tone. I hope that she will stop me, but instead she looks at me sadly and simply agrees, "Okay."

A swarm of conflict flurries inside of me at her passivity. I like to fix problems and talk them through with others. But I am starting to believe that this can't be fixed—especially if no one tries to change it.

Accept the things I cannot change.

"I don't believe in just walking away from problems," I repeat, this time out loud, "but I can't agree with this any longer. I don't know what else to do. Especially after Grandma's funeral yesterday, this is too much for me to handle," I say desperately, the agony too overwhelming to push down. I still hope she will take some sort of action.

"Okay, just text and let me know when you are safe somewhere," Mom says with no emotion.

Courage to change the things I can.

I think of Dad's drug use, the years of alcohol abuse, the fear and manipulation, the rage that only a person like him can feel, and the guilt he puts on us—so much guilt that we don't deserve to feel. Suddenly, and with great clarity, my mind is made up: I am leaving. I don't have a clue where I will stay, but I won't ever come back here.

Wisdom to know the difference.

"Okay," I respond sadly as I turn on the spot, grateful that Dad doesn't emerge from his couch as I walk past. I pass through the kitchen and see the Hamburger Helper on the table for Dad. They sure do remain ever faithful, even if they don't realize it. How fucking fortunate for him. I exit through the kitchen door on the side of the house without saying goodbye to anyone. Getting into my car on this icy Wisconsin January night feels like I have stepped into the middle of the Arctic Ocean.

I throw my small amount of belongings in the back seat. Now that I am finally in quiet solitude, my body relinquishes into a harsh and painful sob, shattering itself from the inside out. Before backing out of the driveway, I look at my childhood home once more and am overwhelmed with grief from not knowing if I'll ever see it again. After a couple seconds pass, I shift my Honda Accord into reverse and leave once and for all.

I do not look back.

CHAPTER 2

MARY:

One sentence can have the power to eviscerate your heart and disfigure your spirit. For me that sentence came eleven days ago: "I am calling to let you know your mother has died." Words that are unambiguous yet cannot be fully comprehended for years, if ever. The thought of moving forward without her both saddens and maddens me in alternating stabs of torment. How can I deeply mourn someone who abandoned my needs in the most appalling of ways? Simply put, because she was my mom.

We were told she had at least six months to live but we barely got two. In those two months she was hospitalized three times, one emergency after another. My adrenaline surged the entire duration. I had things I planned to say to her, writings I wanted to give her, memories I hoped to share. When we got the terminal prognosis, I envisioned a poignant and emotional goodbye that would bring me some comfort. Realizations that should have come out a long time ago would finally break through. I would be vindicated, and authenticity would reign over our family at last. None of that happened. The cancer consumed her quickly and there was no energy for anything except minimizing her suffering.

The funeral was yesterday, and I smile to myself when I think of her resting comfortably in heaven, finally out of pain, and with the God she was so eager to meet all through her life. Even her pastor was impressed with her steadfast faith until her final breath. Just weeks ago, she told me to live fully and lovingly after she passed. After I recover from exhaustion and grief, I intend to do just that. First, I need to heal and get some balance back in my life.

Flashes of my mom's service bring a lump to my throat. It was moving to watch the two granddaughters eulogize her. Katie especially looked at ease in front of the crowd, and I was impressed with what a lovely young lady she has become. At age 22, Katie is the youngest of the three children from my older brother, Ken. I didn't know much about her while she was growing up because Ken wouldn't let me speak to his kids on the rare occasion we were at a family function together. *'They are MY children, Mary. Do NOT talk to them. Do not even LOOK at them!'* he would bellow at me in his overbearing and frightening way.

It was like mental rape growing up with Ken. He was obsessed with controlling me while simultaneously despising me. For his first two years of life, he was the only grand-child on both sides of the family and was revered by every-one. But then my parents sent him to our grandparents' house for a couple of weeks and when he returned home, there I was. They never explained to him about getting a sibling, so when he saw me for the first time, an instant jealousy, rage, and maniacal fixation was triggered that still exists to this day. I had digestive troubles and screamed in pain unless my mom rocked me constantly. She hardly had anything left to give to Ken in those first few years. He thought I was his replacement. His world was rocked, and I was the reason. A compulsion for him to compete with me for our mom's attention became sickly ingrained.

I wonder what is going to happen with Ken now that my mom has passed. She was the primary one who enabled his torturous illness to proliferate all these years. Without that dynamic, maybe he will calm down or go away. Hopefully both.

KATIE:

A shiver runs down my spine as I watch a breath escape my mouth. Even though I have been driving for five minutes and the heat is turned on full force, it's as cold as when I first entered the car. The streets of South Milwaukee are quiet, despite it not even being 9:00 p.m. yet. 'S.M.' never was a loud and festive town, especially not in winter, but now, loneliness and desolation seem to riddle the streets after everything that happened tonight. As I make the turn onto Milwaukee Avenue towards downtown, I realize that I have no clue where to go. I continue on the main strip filled with 'mom and pop' shops on the verge of going out of business, knowing that there is not a destination in mind. I don't know anyone that lives on this side of town anymore since everyone moved away after college. Hot tears blur my vision, and when I almost run through a stop sign, it becomes apparent that I need to stop driving.

Finding a spot on a nearby side street, I pull into it. As soon as I put my car into park, I squeeze my eyes shut painfully, and my head falls back against the headrest. It is times like these that I wish we had cousins, or a reasonable closeness to any of our relatives. The few that we have don't seem to know the extent of our problems. Grandpa surely doesn't, or he wouldn't be throwing away all of his money for his son's addictions. Uncle Stuart, Dad's younger brother by 10 years, still lives with Grandpa and has a tendency to talk to himself at family get-togethers. I'm not exactly sure what is wrong with him, but I do know that he wouldn't be able to help much even if he wanted to. Then there is Aunt Mary, who is nicer than the rest, but always seemed aloof from our family. I am completely stuck.

I pull out my phone to look through my contact list. As I scroll through all the people I know in the area, hopelessness continues to envelope me. A couple friends stand out more than the rest, but I can't find it in me to call them. Try as they might, none of them ever seem to understand the insanity of my family, where the outlandish is our norm, and the unexpected is our expected. I learned early on that our issues seem to stem deeper than most others my age. When I was over at their houses, my eyes carefully observed as I attempted to piece together the picture of what healthy families look like and I would wonder how mine got to be the way it is. I learned that light banter and teasing playfully are okay, but screaming and violence are not. Since most families do the former, I tend to keep quiet about mine.

A particular name stops my thumb from scrolling; it hovers over the 'send' button instead. Do I dare call her? The aloof one? Her mother's funeral was just yesterday. Of all the people I shouldn't dump my problems on, she would be at the top of the list for that reason. Not to mention, I barely know her. I saw her once a year at Christmas and the occasional Thanksgiving for approximately two hours each time. She did say she wanted to keep in touch the night Grandma died, but does that mean for something like this? Can pain ease more pain of a different feather? Or does it become a never-ending loop of pity parties? I wish I knew her better so I could answer these questions.

No, I am not doing it. It's selfish to dump all my problems on my grieving aunt who is no more than an acquaintance to me. No way. I'll figure something else out. As I try to flip back to my contact list to peruse more, my thumb seems to selfishly act of its own accord and presses 'send' anyway.

"Hello?" The confusion in her tone is similar to my own as she answers after a few rings.

"Hi, Mary." That's all I can think of to say at first.

"Hi, sweetie, how are you doing? Holding up okay?" I close my eyes at her question. I don't know what hurts more—the empty hole in my chest from being the outsider or being on the phone with a woman who just lost her mom to cancer and she is asking *me* if I'm okay. I take note of her use of *sweetie,* as if I'm someone who matters to her. Not just the byproduct of her shitty brother.

It hurts. All of it. I try to rein in my breathing to not make her too alarmed.

"Not so good," I say honestly, dipping my toe in the water before diving in.

"Oh, I know. This is such a hard time for all of us. Grandpa and I were talking earlier today about how sad we are to lose her," Mary shares emotionally.

"Yeah," I swallow a lump in my throat. My voice is no more than a croaky whisper. "I know what you mean."

"So what's up, sweetie? Did you just want to talk it out?" Mary genuinely sounds like she cares.

"I—," I hesitate, thinking quickly how to approach what I need to say. "No, that's not all. I hope this doesn't bother you—especially after the funeral—but I was wondering if I could talk to you about something not entirely Grandma-related."

"Of course, what's going on?" Mary is clearly interested.

"Well… I just left my house. There was a big fight." I roll my eyes at the lame description.

"Okay, what happened?" Mary continues to patiently probe.

"It's kind of a long story… and it's about my dad."

"Anything you want to share with me about him, I am open to it. I hope you know that," she responds kindly, and I realize that I *don't* actually know that about her. I don't know *anything* about her, let alone that she wouldn't take any information I disclose and hold it against me. But her tone is far more sincere than any time I have tried to speak to Grandma about Dad's problems. When I approached Grandma Betty about him in the past, I always felt uneasy, like I was apologizing for something *I* did. And every time I actually mustered up to the courage to talk to her, she would tell Dad immediately. His bellows of fury would follow soon after that I was sabotaging his relationship with *his* mother. The fingers surrounding my phone go numb from the cold.

"How much time do you have?" I ask her. My body shudders, either from the freezing temperature or from my adrenaline coming down. I can't tell.

"I've got plenty," Mary encourages me to continue.

"Okay, well to start, I caught my dad ordering illegal painkillers from a street dealer."

Mary gasps sharply. "What?"

"Yeah. It's not the first time either. He abuses drugs from doctors, too. He goes to multiple specialists and gets the same prescription from each of them." I wait for the doubt to come from Mary.

"Wow." She pauses. "When you think he won't go any lower, he just keeps doing it."

For a moment my breath catches, surprised by her response. She actually believes me? I am ready to see how far I can take this.

"Exactly," I respond. "That is why I recorded him doing it this time. I was tired of him always changing his stories when he would do something terrible. None of us ever had anything to prove him wrong before."

"You recorded him? Did you play it back to him?" Her intrigue is growing.

"Yes. And that's where the fight came into play. He was trying to use the money Grandpa gave to my mom yesterday. But he wanted it for drugs, not the bills. I actually stood in front of my mom to stop him and he became furious. He called me a *despicable human being*."

"He what?!" Mary is shocked. "How could he say that to his daughter?"

"Well, he also said I'm no longer his daughter." The sting from saying it out loud stabs me sharply. I close my eyes in attempt to stop the new batch of tears trying to escape my eyes. "So there's that."

"Wow," Mary repeats as she lets out a deep exhale. "I'm speechless. No wonder you are so upset. How did the others respond to that?"

"Sandra and Mom were upset at first but are ultimately turning a blind eye to him. Sandra apologized to *him,* even though we have recordings of it this time. I was so horrified. I had to leave." I hate sounding so weak.

"Where are you now?" Mary shifts to the practical matters.

I let out a laugh, with not even an etch of humor in it. "In my car. Parked outside of a random café in South Milwaukee. I don't know where else to go."

"Are you okay? Do you want to come down here? To Libertyville?"

I feel a swarm of conflict at her question. There is finally someone in the family agreeing with me. Talking to Mary so far has felt like reconnecting with an old friend despite us not having much of a relationship and her being Dad's sister. A small part of me was hoping she would ask that, but as I remember the funeral from yesterday, guilt trickles its way through my body.

"I don't know if I can do that. I feel like I am already burdening you. Plus, I have to work up here tomorrow." Libertyville is about an hour drive.

"Katie, I want you to listen very carefully." Mary is adamant. "You are not a burden on me for this. I have also grown up with him and know how terrible it can be."

Oh. Time pauses briefly.

"He was *always* this awful?" The thought never occurred to me.

"Yes," she responds bluntly. "And he is excellent at turning the rest of the family against each other."

I listen in amazement, as I note that she truly understands how I feel about him. She really gets it. That is his biggest talent—making others blame you instead of him. He creates each and every one of us into the enemy of the given moment, isolating us, and making us feel weak. It's like we have entered Hogwarts; he is Voldemort, and suddenly I have become 'Undesirable No. 1.'

"Okay, I just can't make the trip down tonight because of work tomorrow, but I have an off day on Tuesday." This was my day during the week in which I used to visit Grandma in the nursing home. The lump in my throat is back when I think about her death.

"Tuesday it is. I also think you should tell Grandpa about all of this," she says suddenly, and I am taken aback. That was a known rule with us kids growing up whenever we went to Libertyville: *Smile, pretend you're happy, and don't tell Grandma and Grandpa otherwise*.

"Do you really think I should?" I need confirmation.

"Yes, he is completely in the dark about where his money is going.," she says firmly. "He believes it's for paying the bills for your family."

"That has NEVER happened." Contempt etches itself into every one of my features.

"I suspected that," Mary reveals. "Just come down here and tell Grandpa that; he deserves to know. I'll even do it with you if you are nervous."

I feel suspicious at her urgency because no one in our family ever wants to really talk about this. "Are you sure? I feel terrible about dumping this all on you."

"Seriously, don't ever feel bad for calling me about this sort of thing. I know exactly what you are going through," Mary assures me.

People have said similar things to me before: *'Hey, we'll get through this. Don't worry, we'll do something to fix this.'* With the notches of one disappointment after the other carved into the walls that surround my entire life, it's no surprise that the willingness to believe Mary is waning. But I don't question her more. I'm happy to embrace someone actually listening to me, even if that is all she can do. If we end up telling Grandpa just how fucked up his son is, all the better.

"Okay," I finally agree, and we hang up a few moments later. I rest my forehead on the steering wheel and close my swollen eyes again. At least now there is a plan of action for the next couple days.

My mind drifts back to the literal pile of junk pushed against the wall on my childhood bedroom floor, the one I left only 40 minutes ago. I can't help but compare it to the dark symbolism of our family. There is a pile of figurative junk flying towards us from all directions with Dad at the helm. We briefly speak of getting rid of it, but instead simply push it to the corners of our minds, like the corners of the rooms in the house. The junk is still in our line of vision every day, but out of the way just enough to maneuver through.

My head pounds. I am almost 23 years old with only a few belongings to my name, and I am essentially homeless. For once, I am standing up for myself, like all the childhood book heroes. But I am filled with doubt. If living with the chaos comes with a certainty of having a roof over my head, I can't help but wonder if I am making the wrong choice.

CHAPTER 3

MARY:

I wake up with the usual crook in my neck, forgetting in a split second of bliss that my mom died 12 days ago. I shift a bit in the recliner and pain shoots down my back. I really need to get back to sleeping in a bed. I have been saying this every morning since she got sick. Yet by the time I would get home after sobbing through the dark, cold, late-night streets of Libertyville, it was always the same result. I collapsed into the recliner and passed out instantly, not even getting out of my clothes. Breaking the habit now means admitting that she is gone, no matter how much it is hurting my body.

As I look out the window, I see the sun starting to peek over the vast farm fields next to us. My mom loved all the views from our small and quaint farmhouse no matter what season or time of day. We have had cold but sunny days for a while now, uncharacteristically calm for the end of January, and I'm grateful that the weather did not hold back even one of the hundreds of people who attended the funeral. I think of her with a heaviness that is suffocating. Everyone says it is tougher to lose your mother than anyone else. I'm not sure if this is true but my pain is crippling.

Clarity grips me as I remember talking to Katie. Or was that a dream? I fish out my phone and pull up the call list. *Katie Albrecht, yesterday, 9:02pm, 27 minutes.* The conversation floods my brain, and my heartbeat accelerates as sweat beads dance on my forehead. I had given up trying to make a case as to the depths of my brother's madness because I am a one-man band. It's too exhausting to play the tune on my own. I am shocked to have heard my long-buried words coming out of someone else's mouth last night. Especially his own child's.

My head is murky with apprehension as I plod through my morning routine. Katie said she would come down here tomorrow and expose Ken's lies to my dad. What if she has cold feet? It wouldn't surprise me, but I surely would scream in disappointment. Our family has rules. No one breaks them. We don't talk about the anger, the fear, the violence. We don't talk about our dysfunction. We are ordered to 'keep the peace'. No matter how violent and dangerous Ken's episodes are, we simply must pretend it is not that bad or face persecution. This coping mechanism is cemented into my being from a lifetime of practice.

*****

I'm basking in the sun on this beautiful late summer day in Libertyville. It has been a fabulous few months since graduating from college. My parents' home has become a spa while I recover from the whirlwind of obtaining a four-year degree. Swimming, diving, sunning, biking… it doesn't get much better than this. I have never lived here without him. The bane of my childhood is gone and surely, he won't pose a threat because he is now married to June.

———

Later the same day, as I enjoy a peaceful nap on the living room couch, a phone call startles me to consciousness. My mom's anxiety voice, shrill and piercing, kicks into gear after her initial hello.

"What do you mean you made a mistake?"

The answer comes with a reverberating, menacing tone that invades my sense of safety. A tone that can only come from one person. I quietly pick up the remote and dial down the TV volume.

"Ken… Ken!... stop…. this is irrational. You are not making sense. Are you drunk?" My mom tries to sound tough, but I can hear the fear.

Silence. The phone connects in the cradle. But he ALWAYS calls back. And she unfailingly answers.

"Ken, I'm not going to talk to you if you scream at me," she begins round two of their twisted game of torture calls and hang-ups.

I pull the blanket over my head in disgust as round seven begins.

"I can't believe she would say that to you, Ken. That's horrible. She's not the person I thought she was." She predictably sides with him at some point, every single time.

———

That evening, while reading in my bedroom just at the top of the stairs from our open tri-level house, I hear words from my mom that I thought would never be said again.

"Ken wants to move back home for a while, Arlyn. His marriage isn't working out and it sounds like June is being quite cold. He just needs some time away to clear his head." Her voice is matter-of-fact, as if she's talking about inviting someone over for dinner.

My stomach flips. I tiptoe out to the hall and perch myself at the top stair to get a better listening position.

"Betty, no," my dad says firmly with his usual limited vocabulary.

"You know how sensitive Ken is. I think we should let him know he is always welcome here. God wants us to love him, Arlyn." My mom consistently reverts to the God/love defense.

"Betty, I said no!" My dad stomps down the five stairs to the back of the family room and enters his den, the room where he avoids all the chaos in this household. I hear my mom sobbing in the kitchen.

I bolt out of the back door and go for a run, starting as a jog and ending up in an all-out sprint to command my head to stop screaming at me. I'm still wired when I get back to the house, so I hop on my bike and ride until I can barely pedal. Struggling home with heavy legs, I dive into the backyard pool. As I escape into the abyss of the underwater quiet, my thoughts finally start to clear. Is it really possible that they would allow him to run away from his marriage when he has quit everything else so far in his life? Would they let the neighbors see him living here after they had all been at his wedding? Surely that would be a deal breaker for my mom—letting our family trauma be discovered by the outside world. I assure myself that it's going to be just fine.

"Ken is moving back home for a while," my mom states bluntly as I limp into the house on wobbly legs from my swim. The words crush me like a rolling boulder and I can hardly breathe. My dad is sitting next to her on the couch, staring straight ahead in his usual robotic posture.

"He has a home—a home that you paid for! This isn't his home anymore." I start with logic, hoping to convince my dad. He says nothing.

"This will always be his home, Mary. If we allow you to live here then he gets to as well." My mom's tone has that familiar air of condescension.

"But he is MARRIED, mom!" I hear hysteria creep into my voice. "He only wants to come here because I'm here!"

My insides are convulsing and I become dizzy with emotion. I move from logic to begging. "Please no, please no. Please, mom! Please, dad? When is this torture ever going to stop?" I am screaming now.

"Don't you think you are overreacting, Mary?" My mom still is the only one speaking, but both my parents look at me like I'm pathetic, giving me that demeaning expression of pity I have come to hate.

'Going in for the kill' my mom asks, "Are you on the right medication?" Finding her usual way to make me out to be the crazy one.

My body is on fire and I start to cry, longing for understanding from my parents that he put me through hell. I yearn for them to defend me, to help me, to feel bad for me for a change. Desperately waiting for some words of comfort to come from my mom, she instead says,

"Poor Ken. Nobody wants him. God wants us to love him, Mary. Just be nice to him so that we can keep the peace."

*****

The Fitness Loft, my place of business, is a sanctuary for me. An oasis in the storm. When you walk up the nineteen stairs to the second floor, it's like the rest of the world fades away. It is decorated like a home even down to a kitchen, a shower, and two pet cats—Bernie and Bella. My customers throughout the ten-plus years I have been here are healthy, vibrant, and successful, the type of people I purposely surround myself with to get away from the ugliness I was raised in. And yet here I am, plotting with Ken's youngest daughter to expose his lies, and suddenly his madness is way too close for comfort. My past and present collide.

I need to call Katie, tell her it's not a good idea to come to Libertyville after all. I am nervous as I hit 'send'. I'm about to hang up when a groggy voice mumbles into the phone.

"Sorry, Katie, did I wake you?"

"It's okay. Hold on while I get some water." I hear a faucet in the distance and then Katie is back.

"I'm not going back there, Mary." Her voice is raspy and weak when I ask her how she is feeling about leaving. "It disgusts me." It sounds like she has been crying.

I have been so removed from Ken that I had forgotten how he can twist you up to the point of losing your sense of self, your power, your will. Katie is clearly nearing her breaking point—the electric currents of desperation radiate through the phone. My legs become weak as her emotions permeate my body and release a myriad of frightening memories. I crumble to one of the wicker chairs and pick up a cat for comfort. Do I really want to get involved with this? I've built such a peaceful life staying away from Ken, do I really want jump back into the fire?

I should say I can't handle this.

I should rest and mourn my mom.

I should tell her to work it out with someone else.

"Do you still want to come down here?" comes out of my mouth instead.

Fuck the 'shoulds'. No one helped me and I lost my mind. I don't want that to happen to Katie.

"Yes," Katie says immediately, and we say our goodbyes shortly after that.

I have a pit in my stomach for the rest of the day. I'm nervous and unsettled, yet the situation seems entirely right. Perhaps this is a limb to grab onto, a chance to see the truth for our whole family. Maybe for once I will not be the black sheep, the person seeing the worst in Ken, the problem child because I speak up. After all, my mom and prime Ken enabler, has passed away. Could this be meant to be?

So many disturbing thoughts race through my mind as my childhood comes flooding back to me in waves of panic. I try to nap to clear my head but instead I lay there remembering.

*****

I have a skip in my step as I head home from school because it's been a fantastic day. I'm proudly wearing my cheerleading outfit for the very first time since we are required to do so on game days. Making the freshman "A-team" for football cheerleading is like a dream come true and I am walking on clouds.

'I love my life' I think to myself in the corniest of ways. 'I love high school, I love my friends, I love my hometown.' I start running so I can get home and tell my mom all about it.

As I approach my house my giddiness instantly evaporates when I see the empty driveway where my mom parks. Why is she late again? She promised she would be home on time for once since it is my first Friday night game. A thick knot in my throat impedes my breath and every ounce of me wants to run back to school. It's not good to face Ken alone. But I have to get ready for game night.

Standing on the front porch my mind rolls out repetitive scripts from my mom:

'He's not that bad, Mary. Why are you so afraid of him?'

'He IS your older brother after all. He has your best interests at heart.'

'God wants us to love him, Mary.'

Rolling my shoulders back and standing as tall as possible, I open the front door.

The curtains are closed, the lights are off, the TV is blaring, and it smells like intestinal gas. I gingerly put my backpack down and look into the family room, just five steps down from the front door. He is in his usual spot in the recliner eating his normal stack of at least sixteen pieces of toast and staring at the TV. He has that same greasy headband on, and a t-shirt he's been wearing for days now. It looks like he didn't go to school again. His junior year of high school is starting out the same as all the others.

He looks up at me with contempt.

"Hi Ken," I say. No response.

"What are you watching?" I try again. Nothing.

I shrug and walk into the kitchen.

"Maaaary, get me some orange juice RIGHT NOW!" The command stabs at my senses.

"Okay," I say cheerfully despite the fear percolating inside. The glass I grab from the cupboard slips from my shaky hand and shatters across the tile.

"Q U I E T!" he bellows from his chair.

Trying once more, I pour the juice painfully slow so as to not make a sound and tiptoe down to the room I secretly call 'The Dungeon'. My heartbeat is so loud I am fearful he will hear it. The end table, where he always wants me to place the things he demands, is just beyond my reach. As I lean in to make contact, I accidently step between him and the TV for a few seconds. My breath gets stuck as I gasp.

His explosions are volcanic.

"I told you to never EVER get between me and what I'm watching, you idiot! Why don't you ever listen?!"

His voice rips at my ear drums. I cannot speak; nothing I say will calm him down at this point.

"Answer me, dammit!"

By his tone I know what is coming next and I panic, shooting up the stairs two at a time. I almost make it to the second floor, but he is way too fast and strong for me. He grabs my ankle at the top riser and drags me down face first. I land with a thud on the foyer tile.

"I asked you a question, you fucking moron! What the hell is wrong with you?" He stands over me as I curl up in a ball.

"I'm sorry. I forgot," I say meekly.

"You forgot? You FORGOT? Well maybe this will make you remember…"

He effortlessly scoops me up from the floor despite my struggles to break free and slams me against the front door so hard that I think I'm going to lose consciousness. By the time my vision clears, he has peacefully resumed eating his toast downstairs.

Limping up to my room, whisper-groaning from the pain, I collapse onto my bed and cry.

Dumb... dumb... I am so dumb, I sob into the pillow. Why did I come between him and the TV? That's not too much to ask.

Mom is right.

It is my fault that he gets so mad.

I will get it right next time.

*****

Nausea bubbles within and I start cleaning ferociously, working myself into a sweat. But my emotions don't settle like they usually do when I pull out this coping mechanism that stems from childhood. Back then when Ken would scream, I would clean. He would start in at dinner and I would jump up and do dishes. He would fight in the night with my parents and I would get out of bed and organize my closet. For a teenager, I had the tidiest surroundings of any of my friends. This defense usually serves me well to this day. But not this time. I'm agitated beyond control. I'm not sure I can take this dangerous aberration back in my life.

I go home for CritterFest, another therapy tool I have developed. CritterFest is when I actively play with my animals, exhausting them and me into a peaceful rest. It's a take-off from SummerFest, a huge festival that the city of Milwaukee puts on every year. I have CritterFest built into my iPad calendar with its own special color as a daily repeating event with no end date, rain or shine.

I spend the rest of the evening walking and running my two dogs until they no longer want to move. As they eat voraciously, I bring my two cats outside and follow them closely so they don't get lost or eaten. Tonight is one of those times that they are *'all cat'* and I find myself in the most awkward of places.

Once the cats are feasting on tuna, round two for the dogs begins with ball and stick chases. For the last event of the night, I bring out the fishing line and lure that the cats love, and the fun continues.

I take in the fresh air and drink my usual pale ale. I soak up the simple pleasures that I have created in my life as an antidote to my tumultuous youth. I replay Katie's tension and trauma in my mind and my throat starts to close up. What have I gotten myself into?

I am drinking too much, but I'm not drunk. My adrenaline is high, and my thoughts are racing. I go to bed earlier than usual, hoping to escape the memories for a few hours. Instead, my recurring childhood nightmare permeates my sleep.

*****

It's the middle of the night and I wake up shaking and crying from the nightmare I've had for years. I try my breathing exercises to calm down, but with no luck. It's going to be another rough day at school tomorrow without sleep, especially now that I'm in high school. I close my eyes but cannot shake the image. Ken, barely hanging on at the top of the cliff that he just went over. We are on one of our family outdoor adventures and have lost sight of our parents. As we walk along a narrow and steep trail, Ken disappears from my side. I look to where he once was, only to see a hand holding onto a branch. Carefully peering over the cliff, Ken is looking up at me with pleading eyes.

"Help me, Mary," he begs while reaching up with his free hand.

"I can't, Kenny. I'm not strong enough to lift you. Can't you pull yourself up?" I say hopefully.

He just hangs there looking helpless. "Help me, Mary, help me, Mary…"

"I can't, Kenny. We will both go down. Come on, Kenny—just try to pull up—you can do it."

I look into his desperate eyes. "I'm sorry, Kenny. I can't help you. You are too heavy to lift."

He exerts no effort to save himself. "This is your fault, Mary."

"I'm sorry..." I cry out as he disappears down into the depths of nowhere. No yelling, no sounds, just gone. I drop into a ball on the ground and rock back and forth. Mom and Dad are going to be so mad at me.

And then I wake up. Covered in sweat and shaking just as I've done for years and I'm only 14.

*****

And then I wake up again and realize I am 50 years old and have not had this nightmare for decades.

Until now.

CHAPTER 4

KATIE:

The wail of a familiar jingle jolts my eyes open from the shallow sleep I was momentarily immersed in. The room around me is both recognizable and foreign as my eyes wander over the four corners that inhabit me. My eyes squint painfully as I observe the photographs of a young man and woman, standing together in various locations, on the mantle of the fireplace. These pictures, combined with the brown and black tones of the furniture around me, tell me I am at my brother Josh's place that he shares with his girlfriend, Annie.

I hear the noise again and look down at my phone on the ground next to the bed. It's Mary. She asks something about still coming down to Libertyville. I somehow blurt out a version of yes, groggy from my lack of sleep. With Mary's question, and the heaviness that resides in my chest, I am suddenly reminded why I am here in the first place and that I brought Mary into this mess.

Our conversation is short, much contrasted to the one last night. I can feel pins and needles in my eyes every time I blink. We hang up a few minutes later, after I tell her I need to get to work. I stay on the couch and stare up at the ceiling through clouded eyes. Normally, I would enjoy the stillness of the morning, and the quiet of the empty house, but this morning no peace finds me.

As I glance at the time on my phone, reading just after 9:00 a.m., I reluctantly get up so I can get ready for work. I don't even bother being quiet as I remember Josh telling me that he and Annie would both be out early this morning. They were understanding about why I had to crash here, as Josh knows how our father can be. There were times when I was twelve and Josh was on the brink of leaving for college at the angsty age of seventeen, that he would tell me that he couldn't wait to get out of that South Milwaukee house. *'Once I leave, I'm never coming back,'* he would say confidently.

Only a year later, he did just that—to an extent. He never did move back in with Mom and Dad like he declared, but he continued to live only 20 minutes away. He seemed to change his thought process about them during this time, giving Dad the *benefit of the doubt* more often than I ever could. When I first called him last night, asking if I could spend the night, reluctance poured through his voice. I almost took back my question, ready to shovel those words right back into my mouth and sleep in my car in the freezing temperatures. I pushed aside my hesitancy instead, and he and Annie ultimately agreed with me last night about Dad's problems. The question is, for how long will they continue to do that?

I walk around the corner to the bathroom tucked in the wall on the other side of the stairs. As I look in the mirror, I observe the person staring back. She looks at me solemnly, with giant bags of a purplish color surrounding her eyes. She attempts a smile, and I can feel my lips turning up in return. However, no light reaches her eyes. It's as if a puppeteer stands above her and yanks the corners of her mouth upward, at a total loss of her free will. As they are released, they fall back down quickly, unable to fight the imminent gravity.

I take a deep breath as I pull out my makeup bag. I do my best to cover the obvious signs of trauma, wanting to help that girl that stands opposite of me at least get through the day—yet another day to pretend that everything is alright. She eventually hides her tear-stained cheeks and the bloating around her eyes enough for people to think that maybe she just didn't get enough sleep the night before.

Anxiety floods my chest at the prospect of going into work this morning. I can neither see out of my own eyes nor anywhere into the future continuing in my current role. For nine hours a day, I cold-call to sell home exterior products and services. I am terrible at it. I typically need my thoroughly detailed notes by my side or I panic while I'm on the phone. Not that they actually help, as I still haven't made one single sale in the month since I started this job. If there were ever to be a day when I finally break through and make a sale, it sure as hell is not going to be today. I don't want to accept my fate as the company's worst salesperson, but sometimes it hangs over my head like the inevitable dark cloud of where I come from.

I search through my bag for my work notes. After sifting in between my laptop, other notebooks, books, and even the clothes still packed from Grandma's funeral, I realize they are nowhere to be found. I pull my purse up to my lap to begin my quest through those contents before stopping after only a moment, realizing that the large, bright-yellow spiral notebook would be hard to miss in a one-pocketed purse.

Fuck.

"Fuck. Fuck. Fuck," I repeat out loud. I *need* those notes.

The truth is painstakingly obvious now, and there is no way around it. I let out a coarse breath, trying to reassure myself that I will just duck in and out quickly and avoid all confrontation if possible. My two bags flung over my shoulders, I head to my car on the street. Before I have a chance to change my mind, I put the car into motion towards the place I had sworn off just twelve hours ago. Ten minutes pass and I am pulling up alongside the familiar two eye-sores of bushes placed next to the curb.

In and out.

I dart up the driveway as quickly as I can, hoping that I look more confident than I feel. Sandra sits in the recliner in the family room, watching TV as I come through the door. I keep my eyes glued to the wall near the staircase, determined to not slow myself down or say anything I don't want to. She remains silent as I turn the corner and dash up the stairs. There is a thick tension that lies between us, but I don't know what to do about it. I note the absence of Dad's figure on the couch though, and relief flows through me that he is not here.

The moment I enter my room, my eyes start searching for the familiar yellow notebook. When I don't see it at first glance, I immediately begin digging through the various piles on the bed and floor. I place my phone and keys in a small clearing on the corner of the table next to me, and the search carries on for another five minutes. When no luck is evident, I run my hands through my hair as frustration mounts itself in my chest. Looking at the time, I notice that if I don't leave soon, I will be late for work.

Sadly, I realize that I will have to do without my notes today as I grab my keys. Just before I reach the door, I turn around and look at the tornado that is my bedroom. There are a lot of movies where people have to leave their homes at a moment's notice. I have always wondered why they take the belongings that they do and thought I surely would take more if I were in their place. It would be stupid to leave so many of your possessions behind because you just never know what you are going to need. However, as my eyes travel over the piles of clothes, the keepsakes from my friends, and the photographs, I now understand all those characters in the movies. It is best to part with these items from the past because they represent a life I no longer desire.

I hesitate a moment longer as I continue staring at my room, devouring it. I take a picture in my mind and store the childhood memories that are confined in between these four walls. I silently say goodbye to it before I turn around and carry my feet back down the stairs, listening—cherishing—each individual creak as if it were the last chance to ever do so.

I am almost out the kitchen door when Sandra's voice pauses my step. "I really don't want to leave things between us like this."

I slowly turn toward her and study her face intently. I remember the words she said to me last night, and the implication behind them: *I'm not the enemy here, Katie.* Even though they still place a heavy weight on my shoulders, my hurt from yesterday has already lessened greatly as I see my sister and the remorse pouring visibly out of her.

"It's not you," I respond after a moment, swallowing my resentment. "I just can't take this life with him anymore."

Her head gives a small nod, as if saying she understands, but worry is still etched into her features. The tension lingers. I don't know what else to say.

"But are *we* okay?" she asks.

I am still upset from her turning on me, and I'm on edge for coming back to this house for no reason. I can practically hear the clock screaming at me that my valued time spent here with Dad somewhere else is running out.

"I don't know, maybe we just need some time." I hope that's enough for her to let me go.

Sandra watches silently as I move an inch towards the door, indicating that I need to leave. It would probably be better to stay here and talk it out like the 'adults' that we now are, but the longer I am in this house, the more I can feel the walls closing in on me, like an animal stuck in a hunter's trap.

"Okay," she says, her eyes drifting downward as she does.

It saddens me that I am making her feel bad, but I also am relieved that I can leave before Dad returns. But relief flips to panic as the crank of the screen door sounds to my right. Instantly I am standing just five feet from the man that 'raised' me in this nightmare.

We stare at each other, not dropping eye contact as he continues to block the doorway. My jaw flexes in defense as I feel the hair all over my body stand straight up. The animal trap is tickling my skin as it reaches to wrap itself around me.

"I'm out of here," I say, thoughts of hashing things out with my sister disappearing from my mind as I move to push past him.

He doesn't budge, and my anger heightens. He mutters out an 'I'm sorry,' but he does it with a tone of expectancy, as if he is saying *I did the right thing, now where is my gold star, dammit?* There is no remorse in his eyes.

"It doesn't matter anymore," I say tersely, and I succeed at getting out the door and into my car. It always alarms me how angry I get when I am around him; it seems to crawl its way through my skin. I'm not remotely like this with anyone else. He brings out the crazy in me, and I cannot—will not—take it anymore.

As I try to cool the heat radiating from my center, I look at the clock on the dash, making it even worse. Work starts in fifteen minutes, and it's a half hour away. I reach over to the passenger seat for my phone so that I can let my boss know I'll be late. A few seconds pass as I grab around where my phone is usually placed, only for my hand to come up empty. Agitation floods my chest as I try to remember where I put it. My mind's eye flashes to my end table, how I dropped both my keys and phone there. I stare at the keys in my hand, the only item of the two I had picked back up.

"Oh, come on!" I let out to no one in particular and, before I know it, I'm exiting my car once more. Anger sears through me as I run back up to the house that I keep swearing off forever. Dad sits at the table as I storm through the kitchen door.

"Sit down for a second," he garbles out, his voice slurred from his new round of drugs. "We should talk about yesterday."

"Not a chance," I respond sharply as I run up to the second floor, two stairs at a time. My vision almost blurs, I am so infuriated at him. I quickly grab my phone from the exact spot that I had remembered and rush back down the stairs. I take in a deep breath, knowing I'm going to have to face him one more time. He is ready for me when I turn the corner—he knows the sound each step makes, too.

"You know, you said some terrible things, too." He tries to look hurt as he mumbles this.

A monster inside me that only he brings out roars at his words. *He* was ordering illegal drugs and blamed all of us. *He* told me I was despicable. *He* has abused us all our entire lives. And now he's blaming *me* for confronting him? For wanting him to stop ordering illegal painkillers? Not going to happen.

Rage beyond measure fills me, reminding me how mad at him I have been my entire life. I need to get through to him, but words never do. I need him to feel the pain he has given me. My body reacts instead of my lips as my hand opens and winds up as I am about to walk past him. His back faces me as he continues to grumble angrily. My open palm lands on his back, slapping him, as I continue to the door, knowing that it had no effect on the large mass of his body.

"What was that for?" he demands, still with an ever-present slur in his voice.

"You will not keep doing this to us," I respond heavily as every emotion running through my mind pours out of me and I try to think of something else to say to shut him up.

"What's the matter with you!" he shouts back as I turn in the doorway to lock eyes with him once more.

"I'm telling Grandpa where all his money has been going, and you can't stop me," I say, finally getting the reaction that I was looking for. His face turns from anger to shock as he screams, "Don't bring him into thi-"

I slam the door before he has a chance to finish his sentence.

As I drive toward work, my adrenaline high dissipates, and regret seeps its way through instead. The disappointment from letting myself get as angry as I did relentlessly forces its way past any other emotion. I cannot believe I let him get to me again. In my four years away at college, I worked hard to be a different person. I created an amplified persona for myself around others; I was the one who was always happy, the one who covered up what my childhood was actually like. I thought I was growing—that I had actually become that character. I should have been able to handle his level of crazy and not stoop down to it. I should have been able to live with him on a short-term basis without becoming the person he drives all of us to be. He wants us to be as miserable as he is, and unfortunately, it works most of the time. I can't believe I slapped him, even if it didn't hurt him. That's never been who I wanted to be.

How can I be so confident outside those four walls but weak when I reside within them? I can be there for a matter of hours and find it impossibly hard not to fall back into old habits. When my friends tell me what kind of individual they think I am, they don't realize the baggage that I lug around behind me. They tell me I exude a positive outlook on life, that I am kind. But how can that possibly be true if I can't even get along with my own father? If I was truly who they describe, wouldn't I be able to maintain my emotions with him, too?

I try to push these thoughts away as I continue the drive to my dead-end job. Walking up to the door, I attempt to mentally prepare myself for making those cold-calls and hope that my coworkers can't tell what a mess I am.

———

I am on my third cup of stale, office coffee by the time an hour passes. There is a part of me that thinks the more caffeinated I am, the faster the hands on the clock will circle around to the top. I've made at least ten cold calls at this point, attempting to put my best fake voice forward for the people to whom I have spoken. Can they hear how upset I am? Can they tell how broken of a family I come from? Maybe that's the reason they never buy anything from me.

My cell phone buzzes from the corner of my desk. I grab it and walk towards the break room when I read the name that flashes: *Momma.*

"Hey," I answer.

"Hi Katie, how are you doing?" She sounds like she always does.

"Not that great." I, on the other hand, am very hoarse from crying.

"Well, Dad wants to let you know that he is sorry." She states it like she is talking about the weather.

My stomach knots up. "Does he even know what he is sorry about?"

"Well, just that he made you feel that way. He did sit down and talk to me, you know." An air of superiority surfaces in her voice.

I scoff, "Did he finally admit to buying illegal drugs?"

"No, but he did say that he was trying to help some girl and she was affiliated with bad people. He blocked all of their numbers though." The faithful, yet naïve wife comes out.

"And you believed him?" I can hardly keep from shouting those words.

"I believe that he deleted them, I watched him do it." There is the condescending tone again.

"Look, Mom, I need you to really understand what I am about to say. That was the last straw for me—I am not coming back." I hope she hears the rawness in my voice.

"Okay well, we'll just take it one day at a time," she says, and I once again realize that I am speaking and not being heard.

"No, really, Mom. I'm done. I am not going back . . . ever."

Seconds pass as she seems to contemplate what I've said. She is guarded, and I can tell she doesn't believe me.

"Alright," she says curtly.

Tears brim behind my eyes again, and I suddenly want to tell my mom how much she means to me.

"Mom I—- I love you," I stammer out. None of the Albrechts were ever very good at saying those words and we significantly lacked practice. "I hope you know that he doesn't deserve you."

"I love you, too, but we can discuss this later." She brushes me off again.

"Really, Mom. I do love you. Just remember that the next time he acts out on you."

We end the call with me having a swirl of emotions, twisting their way through me: dejection, anger, and a sharp pang of betrayal that my family would choose a person like him over a person like me. I am starting to feel convinced that I must be the problem after all.

CHAPTER 5

MARY:

Yoga day at the Fitness Loft will hopefully soften my nervousness before Katie arrives. The abundant sunshine pouring through the windows in the expansive exercise room suggests that everything will be fine, yet I am unsettled. It is still possible that she won't show up, or that she won't be as resolute. I'm not familiar with the depth of determination Katie may or may not have, but I do know that up until now EVERYONE. IN. OUR. FAMILY. ALWAYS. BACKS. DOWN. FROM. KEN.

Looking out the front window of my business, I take in the bustling view of a normal Tuesday morning on Peterson Road. Cars everywhere, parking lots filling up, sounds of business and busyness that are comforting to me in this thriving town of Libertyville I have come to love. Despite my history growing up here, I now appreciate what my parents sought after in raising us in a place with this kind of opportunity, this kind of wealth. I try to never take that part of my past for granted. Ken long ago chose to rebel against it, though rebellion is only a fraction of what he has done. I seldom think about what a literal and figurative mess his kids have lived in, but when I do, I know to be thankful that I do not know the full extent of it. He is nothing like the men I know here, who work hard and sacrifice to support their families well, who are groomed and fit and responsible and kind. When I see Ken on the rare occasion that I must, I am constantly shocked at his appearance—disgusting and greasy—wanting to convey the look of a homeless creature or a deranged criminal, or both. No wonder he cannot keep a job. His wife and my parents keep a roof over that family's collective heads. I am fearful of what horrors Katie will reveal when she gets here.

KATIE:

Libertyville. A far northwest suburb of Chicago that is a hop, skip, and a jump from where the Illinois and Wisconsin borders touch on the eastern side of the states. It is a family village filled with wealthy people of the white demographic who seem to have their lives put together. People in these parts sit on their porch swings and watch the neighborhood kids play out in the street, just past their landscaped lawns and manicured bushes. They look across to a similar yard and house, because all of them are well-kept and beautiful. Libertyville is a place where the only crime that takes place is rolling through a stop sign or driving a little too fast. A place where homeowners give out full-sized, full-priced candy bars on Halloween instead of the traditional fun-sized ones. In Libertyville, there is not a single hair out of line on the heads of the residents living the perfect American dream.

Libertyville is where Dad's parents decided to raise their family. We went there a lot growing up. Grandma and Grandpa's house stood out in our minds from the rest of the homes in the area because of its forest green exterior that was so unlike the color palette of creams and grays that filled the rest of the block. They had a kidney-shaped in-ground pool in the backyard that was comfortably heated and always vacuumed of any acorns on the smooth concrete bottom that could potentially bruise our wading feet. Grandpa hired people to keep it swim-ready for our arrival but fastidiously managed the chemical levels on his own. Surrounding the pool was a clean-cut lawn of grass with bird feeders and bushes hugging the edge of the yard line. It was pristine.

The house's interior was always clean due to their hired cleaning people, a Chinese couple that I have seen maybe once or twice growing up. They always nodded and said hello when we would bump into them, but the lack of language understanding from both parties halted any further communication. They steamed and vacuumed the carpets to an even coat of off-white perfection and pressed all of the linens to have exact right-angle corners. Any time my siblings or I spilled the occasional soda or chocolate on those carpets, my grandparents acted like the world was collapsing on itself. With the open floor plan and natural lighting from the living room windows, it's no surprise that Grandma and Grandpa seemed to relish the thought of people looking in and seeing their 'picture-perfect' family. It was a breath of fresh air from the dark carpets and thick curtains constantly drawn at our South Milwaukee house, where no one was allowed to peer in at the destruction that was really us.

Libertyville was like a vacation to us, a vacation that recurred just about every weekend because of Dad's obsession with going there. We would walk into Grandma and Grandpa's house, smile at them, and act like the happy family image we were told to uphold. Mom always said not to fight in front of any of the relatives. 'They don't need to know,' she would say, especially with Dad's parents. We tried our best to live up to their image of us.

Every weekend when we visited, we had two different lives. The five of us would have to separate our minds from being in front of our grandparents versus the ride down there. Car trips were always the worst, because Dad took the fact that we were all in the same moving vehicle, without an escape, as a perfect opportunity to unleash his anger. He sat in the front seat typically, while Mom drove, and would criticize something that we said to him from months or even years previous. Sometimes, it seemed like he raised his voice at us just because he felt like it, and we had no choice but to endure it for the hour down. Even though our voices would be raw from begging him to stop, and our eyes would be swollen from tears, when we arrived at the Libertyville house, our grandparents never heard even a peep of what had just happened.

Sunshine pours into the car from my sunroof window as I drive into this town I've known all my life. I am anxious to meet with Mary. In some ways, it feels wrong to go to Dad's family when he is the person I am avoiding. Mary says they don't get along, but it still seems shameful to tattle to his sister. Even as I pull into the lot of her business, The Fitness Loft, I notice a tremor in my hands from the nerves firing away in my body.

The Fitness Loft is on the north end of Libertyville, about two miles away from Grandpa's house. Its exterior is blue in color and blends in with the rest of the businesses on the block. When driving past it, it may even go unnoticed to the unobserving eye while being mixed in with the air conditioning company, the roofing business, and the cabinet shop that surround it.

Mary texted this morning that she left the door unlocked for me even though her part of the business is closed. I open the door and am immediately surrounded by pale yellow walls and the scents of essential oils from the massage room just at the top of the stairs. I climb the staircase, and my eyes skim over the soothing pastel purple and blue theme and the various trinkets and wall decorations, all having to do with cats in some variation. From paperweights of cats doing yoga to photos of Mary with her actual cats, there is no question which animal breed is her favorite.

On one wall are giant inflatable exercise balls elevated on racks that range from three to seven feet off the ground. Mary uses them with her clients for workouts to activate their core and help them with balance. Underneath the racks are an expansive assortment of brightly colored weights ranging from one to twenty-five pounds, all organized in impeccably neat rows that border the entire wall. Everything about this place is orderly. There is a small kitchen unit with a sink, a blue microwave, a couple of hanging cabinets containing snacks and silverware, and of course, more cat decorations. The rest of the room is encircled by nearly floor to ceiling mirrors, and peeking over the top of them, one can see pastel blue walls. At the end of the room in front of one of the mirrors, there is a stage small enough for only one person to exercise, elevated about a foot off the ground, with roughly fifteen yoga mats folded in perfect squares spaced fastidiously in front of it.

The tag line of The Fitness Loft is *Welcome Home to Health,* and it really does feel like a home. Mary even went as far as getting real cats to live at the Loft only a few months ago. I can see the two of them nestled in the piles of blankets on the stage, now that there is no class going on, taking an afternoon nap.

"Hello?" I call out.

I hear Mary's voice from the back room that she'll be up in a second. I approach the stage and bend down to pet the calico cat named Bella. I feel a quick ache of sadness remembering that the last time I was here on this stage, I had gotten the call that Grandma had passed away.

"Hi, Sweetie," Mary says as she enters the room. She is dressed in a tie dye t-shirt and loose-fitting yoga pants for her small frame. While most fitness instructors display their body with pride due to the years of hard work they put into it, Mary seems to prefer the opposite, swallowing herself in piles of fabric. It makes her very relatable, though I do sometimes wonder why. As she approaches me, I lean down to briefly hug her since she is at least four to five inches shorter than me.

"How are you doing from these past couple days?" she asks with genuine compassion.

I shrug, words evading me. "Do you still want to hear the recordings?"

"Yes, but let me grab a beer first. Do you want one?"

My face breaks into a grin at her question, my first real smile in days. Not only are we at a fitness studio, but it is also like two o'clock in the afternoon.

"Yes, please," is of course my answer.

Mary laughs and walks back to her office containing the mini fridge. The fridge I have since learned contains only beer, wine, and the occasional cheese stick.

"So, have you talked to either of your parents since you left?" she asks as she hands me a pale ale and an opener upon returning.

"Thanks," I say as I pop the bottle cap off. "My mom called me at work yesterday but that was about it."

"How did that go?"

I shrug again, remembering Mom's stagnant mindset. "The same as it was when I left."

I sit down on the stage and pull out my phone. After a couple seconds I am on my recordings screen.

"It's quiet, but I think you'll be able to get the gist of it." I worry that it won't portray how bad it actually was.

"I'm sure it will be fine," she tells me, and I'm surprised again by her patience.

I play her the recordings and show her the videos that I captured. When there is a break in the dialogue, I explain briefly what was happening in that moment. As we listen, I remember again how obvious it was that I was witnessing a drug deal. From Dad asking for *Percs*, to him bargaining the price down for what he was getting, there is no mistaking what took place that night. I silently thank myself that I finally recorded him doing this because it is the proof I need not to fall for his manipulative tricks.

When the recordings end, I start the videos showing Mom, Sandra, and I confronting him. Not much can be seen except the dark silhouette of Dad himself and the occasional glimmer of white from his too-large eyeballs. The audio, however, is clear and crisp. Nausea hits me as Dad's voice bellows through the speaker. *'Give me my damn money!'* I notice once again how his story seemed to change at least four times in the three minute and twenty-two second video. It is no wonder I felt I needed to record him.

"Wow." Mary lets out a long breath when she realizes I have no more to show her. "I had almost forgotten how angry he can get."

"I know. It doesn't even seem real." I sigh with fatigue.

"We have to show this to Grandpa." Mary confirms what she said over the phone.

"How do you think he will respond?" I ask fearfully.

"I think it'll be a shock. But he will be able to handle it. He's a tough guy, your grandpa," she assures me. I want to believe her, but I don't. My grandfather and I never had much of a relationship, having exchanged no more than ten sentences over the span of my entire life.

I decide to change the subject. "I still don't know how I am going to hide from him. I'm terrified that he will come find me at work."

"Hmmm," Mary purses her lips. "Would it be worth it to quit your job?"

"I don't have another job lined up." I never like to be without a job.

"Well, maybe you can start looking today." Mary sounds so positive, unlike her older brother.

"I can try. Would I be able to use your internet?" I only have my backpack and purse to my name, but in those bags are certain necessities like my laptop, cell phone, wallet, and even my Social Security card. It seems like the stars are aligning. I have always carried so much with me for so long, and now it seems it was needed for this unexpected moment in my life. I don't have everything, but it's everything I need for now. Everything I need except my—-

"Shoot, my phone charger," I say aloud.

Mary looks at me, perplexed. "What about it?"

"I left it at work, and my phone is about to die." This is the worst time to not have an accessible phone.

"I'd give you mine but it's an iPhone." Mary lifts up her phone to show me.

"I guess I'll have to buy another one," I say and try not to panic at my soon-to-be decreasing bank account. Right then, the massage therapist who rents out space from Mary comes out of her room as a massage just ended. Mary looks over towards her.

"Sheila, do you happen to have an Android phone?" Mary asks her.

"I do actually!" Sheila says in a cheery voice. "I have a Samsung S5."

I am relieved as I hold up my phone so Sheila can see it's the exact same one in her hands. Usually I have trouble finding someone with the same charger.

Maybe I do have luck after all.

Mary:

I walk to the other side of the Loft while Katie charges her phone, plunk onto the stage, plop my head on one of the cat's beds, and close my eyes. I've been trying to be strong for Katie but hearing Ken's voice on the recordings terrified me. I knew from the second I came out from the back room and saw Katie's demeanor that this was going to be awful. Despite the limited contact I've had with her through the years, I think of her as upbeat, full of life, confident, and smart. She enters a room with impact due to her height, physical beauty, and magnificent smile, greeting everyone with direct eye contact and positivity. Today there was no smile. In my recent but now usual coping style I instantly decided the moment she arrived that it was time for a beer, even though it was only about 2:00 in the afternoon. I was pleasantly surprised that Katie agreed to join me.

I sit up now and look to where Sheila usually sits and see that she and Katie are deep in conversation. Katie is facing me but unaware that I am staring at her, taking it all in—her recordings, her words, her pain. The look she has is familiar, a combination of fire and disgust, strength and fear. My mom always told me that Katie is the one in the family who causes trouble for her parents. She is the one with the temper. The one who is always wrong and whose life is messed up. She is aloof and on edge most of the time. This is what I've heard for years. *'Katie is really giving them grief,'* my mom would say. This description forges to the front of my mind and clashes with the fact that Katie just spoke the most coherent truth that I have ever heard from anyone in our family.

Time stops for a moment as full comprehension floods my brain.

She isn't the problem child at all.

I am now certain she never was.

She is the one speaking the truth.

She is the one who cannot and will not take his crap. She is me.

*****

I'm finally home from another long day in the life of a straight-A high school student and athlete. My days go on forever between practice and meets and homework. I'm so tired I can hardly move, but I put on my cheerful face as I always do. I cannot and will not show any signs of being like Ken. My parents say we are similar. 'You have problems, too, Mary,' they admonish when I complain about him. I am driving myself into the ground by chasing achievement and perfection, even though behind closed doors I am a wreck. But I will never let anyone see my sick side because then what my parents say will be true.

"Hi, Mumzie!" I yell out when I first step foot in the door.

"Hi, Mairzie! How was your day, dear?"

"It was fantastic. I got a perfect score on my math exam and took first place in both my sprints at the track meet." I always list off my accomplishments at the end the day.

"That's wonderful, honey! Are you hungry? There are leftovers from dinner in the refrigerator."

I practically skip over to get the food out. I just love this part of my day. I love my mom and the friendship we have. "I also got a lot of praise for the speech I gave and…"

"Shuuuuuuut the hell upppppp!" Ken's nasty voice bellows up from the family room just across the foyer. I instantly freeze. My mom says nothing as I hold my breath and wait.

"You are such a spoiled princess with all your bragging. I don't want to hear it!" he shouts from downstairs but does not budge.

"I can talk if I want, Ken. This is my home, too." These words tumble out of my mouth almost involuntarily.

"Mary, be quiet," my mom hisses. "Just leave him alone."

"Why do I have to be quiet? He's the one who started it." I'm on a slippery slope now, unable to stop plummeting.

"Mary, please, you are going to ruin the evening. Please let it go." My mom is more angry with me than with him by her tone.

"Why is it ME who is going to ruin the evening?!" The familiar craziness strangles me. "I'm sick of you, Ken," I shout louder so he can hear me clearly. "Just stop. Just go away. I'm talking to Mom, and it's none of your business!"

I feel the stairs reverberate from his heavy stomping. It takes him seconds to tower over me at the kitchen table, and I can smell his nasty breath.

"You heard MY mom, she told you to shut up. Are you going to listen for once in your life, you little bitch?" He jabs at my neck repeatedly with his long, thick, dirty nail.

"YOUR mom? She's my mom, too, and she didn't use those words." I am screaming now.

"Mary, stop it," my mom begs.

The insanity in my head is unbearable. Why am I supposed to stop it? Why isn't she defending me?

"Answer me or else!" He's a rabid animal now. I've gone too far.

I scoot under the table, the only means of escape, and run up to my room, barricading the door with the chair that is always ready for this purpose. His gorilla-like steps shake the house as he storms up the stairs. Within seconds he is pounding at my door.

"Get out here, you stupid coward! Apologize to my mom and me for once in your pathetic life!"

I say nothing. Crawling under the covers, I assume the fetal position and try to control my breathing so I don't pass out from fear.

The rumbling of the garage door distracts him. Dad is home. Ken instantly retreats to his room. Thank God Dad still has some power over him.

My mom is sobbing in the foyer when my dad comes through the front door. "What did I ever do to deserve TWO children who can't get along in the world?" she immediately whines to my dad.

I put the pillow over my head and press it to my ears. I want to scream, I want to run away. I am NOT like him. I am NOT. Don't all of my accomplishments make that clear? And how does not getting along with him equate to how I am with the rest of the world? I am simultaneously furious and sickened to be compared to him.

Pulling the covers tighter, I try to comfort myself. I lie there for what seems like an eternity and constantly assure myself that I did nothing wrong.

I am NOT going to feel bad....

BUT... I did egg him on.

I just wanted to tell my mom about my day....

BUT... I should have just ignored him.

My stomach is doing gymnastics as guilt encroaches about my mom hurting downstairs.

Maybe I am just as bad as him. Why couldn't I just stop talking when they both told me to do so?

I really am a loser.

I quietly open my bedroom door and tiptoe down into the kitchen. My dad is nowhere in sight and I'm relieved that Ken isn't either.

"I'm sorry, Mumzie." I plop onto the chair directly across from her. Her eyes are bloodshot from crying and she looks so very defeated. "I'm sorry I didn't rise above like you always say."

"This is very hard on me, Mary. You need to think of that sometimes."

"I will, Mumzie, I promise. I'm sorry to be so selfish."

She looks at me with genuine emotion, like something comforting is about to come from her heart. I am hopeful she will help me feel better. The words that follow do anything but that.

"I think you owe Ken an apology, too".

*****

I shudder from the memory. It seems like a different person in these images; the weak, good little girl persona I used to be. I hate that girl; she is insulting to my senses. I buried her after years of therapy, managing to get so strong that returning to Libertyville was possible after a long time away. I put mechanisms in place to keep space from Ken while still being part of the family. I would hear of all the chaos he created from a distance, and even with my mom's skewed and always understated relay of events, he seemed so ridiculously out of control that I could hardly wrap my head around the passive acceptance. But I stopped trying to be an agent of change since the dysfunction was an immovable wall. I simply stayed separate, even while in the same room. I had to be careful, though. He would follow me, try to corner me, try to get to me—and he often did. Only a few minutes alone with him would be so sinister I would start to regress immediately. And no matter how calm my exterior appeared, I was always shaking from the inside out in his presence.

I thought the era of Ken being the center of our existence would end after my mom's death. Even though she tried at times to leave him out of our relationship, there was always that cliché 'elephant in the room' that ultimately took up too much space. I loved her, though, and we had a fabulous friendship despite the elephant. I came to see her for the beautiful lady she was to everyone around her, how she was respected by others while maintaining humility. She had myriads of friends from diverse circles and could relate to all of them in depth. She was beloved.

I knew at the deepest part of her core that she was mortified to have a son like Ken. But there was always a rational enough excuse to ignore his eruptions, and I believe she truly felt that by keeping the peace and getting through another day, the problem would eventually go away. But then days turn to weeks, months, years, decades, and the problem becomes so huge, the most giant elephant in existence, that to admit you should have done something at the start would negate most of your life and the choices that were made.

Am I entering another era with Katie here where Ken will once again be the animal stomping on us? Should I put a stop to this? But it feels good to have an ally—I am already lapping up the vindication like a thirsty puppy. Katie is so incredulous, so ready to speak the truth, but at a loss as to how to proceed with our family laws of denial. The laws that were my mother's default, no matter how egregious the situation became.

But my mom is no longer here.

And Katie is.

CHAPTER 6

KATIE:

The car ride over to Grandpa's house is quick but also seems to last forever. I feel every bump from my shocks attempting to absorb each divot in the road. It's been only three days since I've been to his house—after the funeral took place. There were a lot of people then—Grandma's family from northern Wisconsin all drove the distance so we could mourn and celebrate her together. They were a welcome distraction from the emptiness filling that now-desolate house as we all drank our souls out, in what Grandma's siblings would call a 'true Palecek fashion'.

Mary is supposed to be behind me, but I lost her car somewhere along the way when several others wedged themselves between ours. I have always been known for my lead foot when it comes to driving, my two speeding tickets and several warnings are my souvenirs for such a reputation. Knowing that I won't enter that house without her, I will have to wait outside. I make a right turn onto Grandpa's street and am immediately hit with a sad nostalgia at the sight of the forest green house that had once been our escape.

My eyes drift to the lawn in front of it and with a pang in my chest, I remember all the games we used play there. Every Thanksgiving it would be football, Dad always the leader. To make the game fair, Josh and Dad had to be on separate teams, leaving me with Dad, and Sandra with Josh. We'd sometimes enlist the neighbor boys to join us, making it a three-on-three game. '*You're tough as nails, Katie*', Dad would say to me as he coached us in our 'huddle.' As much as I didn't want to admit it to others, I secretly adored his praise. It didn't come nearly as often as the insults, so when it did, I bathed in it quietly.

After a minute or two passes, Mary's Camry pulls in behind me, and we walk up the steps to the house. As we enter the foyer, I immediately feel an emptiness that comes with Grandma no longer being there. Usually when my family would visit, she would be sitting at the kitchen table playing solitaire and would call out '*Hello?*' as if she weren't expecting us to come over. We would always respond with a cheery '*Hi!*' then take off our shoes and join her in the kitchen where we immediately rummaged in the pantry for food.

No such greeting comes this time.

Mary and I call out instead, and I feel like a foreigner in my once native land. Grandpa mumbles something from his den downstairs and makes his way up to greet us.

Grandpa is known for being well put together. Even though his posture is starting to curve in his old age, his gait is still stable and strong. He is the type of person who clearly shows he is wealthy, even to those who don't know him. He comes up the stairs in his typical lounge around the house clothes—slacks and a button up. He is even wearing a belt and Rockport shoes. The thought of wearing a belt and shoes in a place where you would like to feel most comfortable baffles me. I could never do the same.

However, as he comes closer, I begin to notice the cracks in his 'everything is perfect' facade. His head hangs lower, and his eyes seem more tired. This once powerful man is broken down into pieces from the death of his wife. From his demeanor, I am reminded again that I am causing trouble where I shouldn't be.

"Hello," he says to us both.

"Hi, Dad. We are here to chat about Ken like I mentioned on the phone." Mary gets right to it.

He nods silently as his eyes slowly switch over from looking at Mary to landing on my face. "Shall we sit in the living room?"

We make our way to the furniture dressed in a green floral pattern. Grandpa sits in one of the plush rocking chairs while Mary and I sit on the couch. Once we are all situated, Grandpa stares at me expectantly without saying a word. Under his gaze, I feel nervous. My hands grow fidgety and I try to avoid direct eye contact. I don't even know where to begin. How does someone break the news to a man that his son has been terrible to the family he was supposed to protect? Will he even believe me?

Mary seems to notice my hesitation and speaks for me. "Katie came here to tell you about some of her concerns about Ken. She has a lot to show you."

Grandpa nods again as his look intensifies. My pulse hammers at a quickening rate. I look over at Mary, and she tells me it's okay and encourages me forward. I take a deep breath to settle my nerves before finally speaking.

"I-I recorded my dad ordering painkillers from a street dealer," I manage to stutter out even though it makes me out of breath. "He has done it before. A lot. And he uses the money you give him."

Grandpa remains silent as I continue my tale of the past few days. Mary fills in gaps that I have forgotten about in the nervous moment. She probes me to tell the bad parts about how he called me a *despicable human being*, how he screamed in my face saying that I am no longer his daughter. She also tells him that the money he'd been giving my dad to help pay our bills over the years has been fueling all of his addictions like alcohol, drugs, and gambling. I am relieved when she takes over. I have never been good at talking about these things, letting the fear of sounding too victimized take over instead.

After prefacing with the background story, I play the recordings for Grandpa. Grandpa huddles close to the phone to hear better, his hearing aids only doing so much.

His eyes close and remain that way far after the recordings end, stress etched into his features.

He stays quiet for several minutes after we are done, and I start to wonder if he has fallen asleep. Eventually, without saying a word, he gets up, walks into the kitchen, and lets out a deep sigh. I glance over at Mary, trying to figure out why he left. Does he not believe us? Was this too much for him?

"I think this is a good sign," Mary says to me as he turns the corner into the kitchen.

My eyebrows raise in surprise. "Why did he walk away then?"

"He just needs to process things, but he definitely gets it. You are doing a good thing by being here," she adds as she seems to notice my skepticism. After such a build-up, I can't help but think the result is rather anticlimactic.

Mary checks the time on her phone and says she needs to get going. I walk toward the foyer with her and suddenly realize that I still need a place to stay tonight. I was hoping that I could crash somewhere here in Libertyville, ideally at Mary's house since I feel the most comfortable around her. The offer doesn't come though, and I don't want to ask. I consider sleeping in my car again, rationalizing that when you are freed from the captor that controls you, you lose the comfort of a roof over your head.

Fortunately, Mary asks Grandpa as he joins us if I could stay the night here instead.

"Yes, of course. I'll check the room," he responds quietly and then slowly treks up the stairs. I watch each step he takes and feel relieved at his answer. Maybe letting me stay is his way of telling me he isn't upset at me for slandering his son.

"I really do think it is good that you are here. I can feel a shift with our family," Mary says to me when we are alone again.

"I hope so," I respond quietly.

"Really, I believe that. I think Grandma is pulling some strings from Heaven right now to help us. By the end of her life she was completely fed up with Ken but didn't have the energy to stand up to him. You do, Katie. *You* are the chosen one in this family."

My mind immediately drifts from all the 'chosen ones' I have read about over the years. Harry Potter and Luke Skywalker are the first to come to mind from those of the fictional worlds. Their bravery was resilient and their glory was triumphant. It was thrilling to imagine a world like that for myself, but when I pictured it, I only pictured the view from on top of the mountain, not the exhausting, battle-driven climb it took to get there. I ignored how those heroes lost people they loved and were looked down upon by their societies for a long time. They made it look easy to hold on to their beliefs even though their world could literally be crumbling around them.

I am not as brave as my childhood heroes, but I don't correct Mary when she seems so hopeful. Those characters were brought to life in the span of three-hour films or 900-page books, and both are likely to have a happy ending through all the conflict. Those characters are guaranteed to get the glory, while I get persecution from my family. But being that this is real life, there is no guarantee how this story will end.

CHAPTER 7

KATIE:

The Libertyville house has two guest rooms, four bedrooms in total. I have stayed in both of the spare rooms over the years depending on how many people I came with. The one that was Dad's room growing up was bigger and also remodeled recently, making it the more desirable to stay in. Whenever it was all five of us that visited, my parents slept in there, leaving Sandra and me in Mary's old room, and Josh on the couch. However, whenever it was only us granddaughters, we would be the priority to take the nicest of the lot.

Now that everyone has gone to bed and Mary has left for the night, I make my way to 'the more desired' room. Looking around at the two twin-sized beds and other décor, nostalgia blankets me as I realize how much of Grandma is in this room and how much I miss her. Glancing at the bed along the left wall, I am brought back to when I was sick and she hugged and coddled me there until I fell asleep. My heart clenches at the reminders of her everywhere.

I let out a deep breath as I close the door and make sure to lock it behind me. The locks here aren't very secure, but something about the action makes me feel safer, if only by a marginal amount, just in case a certain someone tries to burst through the door at any moment. I try to push that anxiety-producing vision out of my mind as I reassure myself that even though Dad may assume it based on what I said to him when I left, he doesn't know I am actually here. Apparently, he called Grandpa just before I arrived and asked about me. Grandpa didn't know that I would be arriving at that point.

Tomorrow, I am going back up to Milwaukee and quitting my job on a whim. Mary and I discussed it, and it seems like the best option at this point. I can't stay in that area and risk him seeing me around or having him come to my work. It is imperative that I keep distance from him so he can't sway my mind into his beliefs again. And maybe, just maybe, he will realize I am serious this time and get himself some help. I can't believe I would quit my job without a backup, but something about hanging around Mary makes me feel safe enough to trust her judgment.

I climb into the bed along the right wall, feeling like a meatball being stuffed into a hot pocket from the tightly tucked sheets. I try to still my whirling mind. As I prepare for a restless night, I am hit by the irony of the situation: I am staying in a house occupied by two men that I have never had a relationship with, in the old bedroom of the exact person I am on the run from.

Surprisingly, sleep comes easier than I expected.

———

I wake up early the next morning to the smell of coffee brewing in kitchen, most likely the brand Folgers. The scent brings me comfort from its familiarity. I never actually drank coffee here growing up because to my young mind it was bitter and 'yucky', but the scent represented mornings at Grandma's house so I always enjoyed that part.

I check my phone and see yet another text from Dad. He has been texting me non-stop the past few days. I have ignored most of them, knowing that they aren't usually logical.

Ken: Katie, we are having a family meeting at 6:30 tonight. Be there, and we will discuss everything.

This time I decide to respond.

Katie: Did you admit to Mom about buying illegal drugs yet?

Ken: What are you talking about? There are no illegal drugs. 6:30 tonight. Be there. This is important.

His denial causes an angry heat to trickle its way to my face.

Katie: Then I don't see a need to come. And I have a recording of you Dad. Don't lie.

I disregard his next texts, in an attempt to calm myself down again. Normally, his words would play an influence on me and my decisions, but I'm not letting them this time. I unconsciously tighten my grip on my phone that holds all of my proof against him, and therefore every ounce of my confidence.

When I make my way down to the kitchen, I find Grandpa is sitting at the table with a glass of orange juice and a cup of coffee, the morning newspaper in his hands. This was his routine when we were growing up, too; the only difference is the seat across from him typically occupied by Grandma is now empty. He looks up at me as I walk in.

"Hi," he says as he studies me, and I shift uncomfortably under his gaze.

"Hey, Grandpa."

Silence. This is awkward.

"There is some coffee if you'd like," he finally says after a few seconds, eyes glancing over to the counter.

"Sure, that would be great," I say as I momentarily break the heavy tension to grab a mug from the cabinet. "Hey, thanks again for letting me stay over. I appreciate it."

He nods in response. "Your dad called again this morning."

I feel my muscles tense in anticipation as I finish pouring the coffee. I turn around to look back at him, pushing down the anxiety and fear that is rippling through. "Oh?"

"He was wondering if I had heard from you," he says as he continues to study my reaction. I wonder where he is going with this. He had promised last night to not disclose where I am. Did he change his mind and rat me out already?

"What did you tell him?" I ask, trying to keep my tone light and non-accusatory.

"That I have not heard from you," he says simply, and my muscles relax. I am safe for another day.

"Are you ever going to talk to him?" Grandpa's tone is judgmental.

I hesitate with my response. Do I want to talk to Dad? Not until he gets his act together. But I can already hear the protests from the rest of the family:

He is still your father, Katie. Ignoring the problem doesn't make it go away.

Instead of telling Grandpa this outright, I decide to tread carefully. I don't want him to think I handle every conflict in a rage like my father.

"I don't know. We have been hurt by him recently and, quite frankly, as long as I can remember. I do not want to tolerate it this time without any change," I say directly, needing to make sure my intentions are clear to not let this problem just blow over. "That being said, I don't expect anyone else to do the same even if I think it is the right thing to do."

He simply nods again. Perhaps he understands that I am telling the truth. Where it goes from here, I have no idea.

After I gulp down my coffee and finish a bowl of cereal, I climb the stairs to the guest bedroom and once again pack up all of my possessions. I make my bed perfectly, no wrinkle or crease evident, just as Grandma had always done it. Once I finish, I give a final glance to make sure nothing is out of place. I take in the tidy vision before me and feel confident that it looks like I have never been here. Slinging my oversized backpack over my shoulders, I grab my purse and go back downstairs. After thanking Grandpa once more, I leave the house to head up to Milwaukee to quit my job.

CHAPTER 8

MARY:

In the early morning quiet, I momentarily forget what is happening with my family. But then reality hits and my stress response kicks in before I've even moved. It seems like my mom's funeral was months ago, not the mere five days it's been since we said our goodbyes. I'm continuously apprehensive about getting involved with Katie and her father. Her father, my abuser, the one person I never wanted to be near in any way again. Yet every time I see Katie in front of me, I see myself at her age, just as lost as to how to combat the beast, just as horrified that this is actually who and what he is. I remember the day the full revelation hit me that I was physically related to this creature, and it disgusted me to the point of questioning everything I was as a person, because there must be some of him in me.

It took me so very long to realize that people other than my parents do not think I am dark and twisted like him. In fact, all indications have been that what I am is just normal. Humans are allowed to have bad days, to say the wrong thing, to get angry, or to experience any other myriad of emotions without being a narcissistic, manipulative sociopath. It's a shame that I didn't truly feel that until the recent decade or so. If I could help Katie to get to this place of serenity sooner, then perhaps it's worth the risk of confronting what most assuredly will come from Ken.

Since having come out of the shadows of secrecy that my childhood demanded, I have found that profound openness is almost an addiction. My 'editing skills', I am told by my customers, could use some work. Usually they are expressing this in an endearing way, because they say I am unique and refreshing more often than not. I have been blessed by a community of enormous support throughout my years in business. This has been proven by the fact that my customers, sweetly coined my 'peeps', have instantly embraced Katie as worthy and loveable, simply because she is my niece. The outpouring of acceptance and offers to help is astounding to me because, even with my unedited self, I had barely tapped into the extent of the abuse from Ken when sharing with them. Yet they remain faithful and kind despite what Katie continues to reveal.

Arriving at the Loft for my morning classes, I once again experience that wave of peace as I reach the top of the stairs. I am so lucky to have this bastion of sanity that simultaneously grounds me and lifts me up so that I can do some positive work with my life. I'm a long ways away from that insecure, weak, and voiceless girl that my family dynamic made me become. Am I strong enough now to enter back into the absolutely ridiculous world of Albrecht doctrines? In only a few days I am a nervous wreck.

All thoughts of trying to distance myself from the situation evaporate as my peeps begin to arrive. They immediately ask about Katie. I see by the warmth in their eyes that they are already collectively in deep to help this young lady.

"How's Katie?" several peeps ask at once.

"She's okay, considering. She stayed the night at my dad's house," I tell to the group.

"Is she coming here for class today? I have some thoughts that may help," another peep asks.

"Actually, she is on her way up to Milwaukee to quit her job. I encouraged that because her father knows where she works."

"Good call. She needs to be around you, Mary," a third peep chimes in.

"I think so, too," I say assuredly despite my doubts that this will be okay for ME.

"Does she need work? I could use someone to house and dog sit fairly regularly," peep number four offers.

"I think she would love that! I will ask her later tonight. She is meeting us for dinner."

And on it goes, everyone coming together to brainstorm how they can help.

———

That evening, as I sit at an Italian restaurant with my brother Stuart, my dad, and my husband Terry, I can't keep from hoping that Katie will make it back from Wisconsin and join us like she thought she might. Even though there is a thread of tension between us given the topic that has brought us together, I feel differently when I'm around her, like maybe there doesn't need to be that thread at all. Looking diagonally across the table I see Stuart is exhibiting his usual quirks of odd facial gestures and bodily ticks while carrying on a conversation with, according to him, 'someone who exists, but is not actually present'. To the right of me is my dad, a man I've barely conversed with my entire life. He must be grieving horribly for my mom, but I cannot get him to share anything emotional. Sharp pain seers through my heart as I realize I no longer have a family member I can talk to in depth like I used to do with my mom. I wonder if anyone will fill that role again. Across from me is Terry, my wonderful partner in life for over two decades, my protector, my voice of sanity and wisdom when it comes to the Albrecht disease. I'm surprised he stuck around early on after learning the depths of the illness; some of the details are so disturbing I never thought anyone would want to be remotely near me as part of the family. He consistently pulls me back from losing my mind, telling me I'm better than all of it and really wishing I would distance myself more. I'm fearful that with Katie's arrival I'm doing just the opposite.

Terry is attempting to keep the mood light with his sense of humor, but still the night feels as cold and dark as it is outside in this month of January. I question why I even suggested this outing, and the only reason I can come up with is to keep myself busy, and my dad and Stuart occupied, so we don't drown in sadness. My wandering thoughts are interrupted when suddenly Katie slides into the booth next to me. As usual she has that bright smile and cheerful hello even though I'm sure she had a very hard day quitting her job up in Milwaukee. Instantly my spirits lift now that she is here. I'm not ready to let my guard down just yet, but there is something about her that makes me feel at ease. We start up our usual banter as I slide my Pinot Grigio over for her to sip, given that she forgot her ID in the car. I really hope I'm not mistaken about Katie's resolve to continue speaking the truth about her dad and the sick family dynamic he has perpetrated on all of us. My gut instinct tells me I'm not and that she is just what this family needs.

KATIE:

As I take a seat in the booth at the restaurant, I notice that everyone seems to be in good spirits. Grandpa, Mary and I are three sardines in a can on our side, while my uncle Stuart and Mary's husband, Terry, are across from us with at least a couple inches separating them. The waitress politely asks for my ID when I try to order the same glass of wine that Mary has in front of her. I am embarrassed when I realize I left it in the car, but I don't go out to grab it. I parked on the far end of the parking lot, and the daunting coldness in the outside air keeps my butt firmly planted.

When the waitress walks away, Mary slurs out in a whisper that I can have some of hers. After I thank her she shrugs her shoulders and grins, "I've already had a full bottle at the Loft before I got here." I laugh and take a swig of her wine in response. After the long day I've had, wine is welcomed in any fashion. Mary and Terry seem to be keeping the conversation going, as they are the most talkative. I chime in when I can but realize quickly that I don't have to if I don't feel like it. There is an easiness that comes with this group that is surprising. I find them as the perfect company after traveling up north to quit my job.

I didn't divulge too many details when I told my boss I was leaving. I phrased it as an emergency that happened in my life that is causing me to relocate out of the area. It was easier than I expected, and he was very understanding. I even joked that it's probably a good thing for the company since I wasn't making any money for it anyway. It was confirmed true when he laughed and didn't correct me.

Even though I try to enjoy the evening, a million thoughts are racing in my head as to what is the next step for me. I have been considering a move to Madison, in the southern central part of Wisconsin. I have a lot of friends there, and it was where I thought I would end up when I was in college. If I go there, I can be off the grid from anywhere the family lives and won't cause any more problems. As of now I have done the opposite, crossing the Wisconsin border into the heart of where our immediate relatives reside.

The evening continues at the same light-hearted level. I look around and observe these people, my family, that I barely know. From the limited time I have spent with them, I notice the same idiosyncrasies that they have had at family get-togethers growing up. Terry is making goofy one-liners after everything we say. He had a reputation with my siblings and me for his jokes that none of us knew how to respond to. We would laugh politely, but our confusion was always evident on our faces despite our best efforts to conceal it. Maybe I just need a laugh, or maybe it's Mary's second glass of wine that she has slid over to me, but tonight I genuinely find his jokes funny.

Stuart, on the other hand, is talking to himself while the rest of us talk to each other. He has done this since we have known him, but we were told not to confront him—another thing we were supposed to pretend was okay. Since we weren't allowed to talk about it, we just coined him as 'the weird uncle' to those who would meet him. I don't say much to him tonight.

Grandpa isn't saying a lot, but then again, he usually doesn't. I am grateful that he isn't staring at me inquisitively like he was doing this morning. He seems to be content listening to the conversation around him. Every so often, he will drop an uncharacteristic quip into the conversation. When the waitress asked if he wanted regular coffee instead of decaf, he responded: *Sure, I'll live it up!* He even offered for me to stay the night at his place again, which I gratefully accepted.

And then there is Mary, who has been my biggest ally so far. She has been drunk every time I have seen her this week but validates everything that I tell her. I am glad she is here because I wouldn't feel comfortable with these three men otherwise. She is the glue keeping us together.

How did I get here with this group of people? Grandma was always the one I had the biggest connection to, and now that she is gone I feel awkward, despite their calming presences. They are all so welcoming, but I am still getting to know them. I can't help my mind from drifting to Mom and our relationship. We had been getting so close this past month while I was living at my parents' house. And even though I have been somewhat independent for the past few years since going away to college, Mom was always there for me in the times when I needed some support emotionally or financially. I have typically tried to rely on myself, since I learned early on that I could not count on Dad, but as a broke college kid, sometimes I needed a little help. She did her best to come through in those times. I hope we can figure out a way to have a relationship even though I am not taking any more of Dad's bullshit. In the meantime, I can't deny the overwhelming sense of family that comes with the group in front of me. They aren't perfect, and there is still a fumbling grace period that comes with the newness, but they accept me despite the uncertain map of my future and, for the moment, I am grateful for that.

*****

The woods surrounding me are quiet. I hear the crunching of twigs and leaves beneath my feet as I walk. One foot. Two feet. Crack. Crack. Crack.

This is a normal day for me. These woods are familiar and mysterious at the same time. Typically, I see plenty of other people here. Not today though.

My phone rings. I swiftly answer it, fingers gliding over the phone buttons.

The voice is a female—strong and familiar, a friend. The face is unclear in the screen, but I trust her. She says she has an idea for all this, that I should meet her at her house as soon as I can.

'I can keep you safe,' she tells me just before disconnecting. I don't understand her. Why do I need to be safe? But then I feel it. I can't quite place it exactly, but danger looms. It presses on me, a heaviness I could never prepare for. I need to find my friend.

I slip effortlessly through the empty woods until I reach my front door. I grab a few things, then I'm out the door again. I can feel it still, the darkness. It surrounds me. I pick my feet up, willing them to move faster.

'I can keep you safe.'

I have to find her before IT gets me. It's chasing me now, getting closer and closer. I try to pick up my pace to get away from it, but it engulfs me. It's everywhere and nowhere all at once.

It's closing in on me, I'm losing hope.

*****

My eyes shoot open, my heart hammering in my ears. I look around the same guest bedroom of Grandpa's house that has been my home the past couple nights. I take in what I just saw in my head and the anxiety I still feel at this moment. The voice keeps playing in my head:

'I can keep you safe.'

I don't even know who that was. A faceless figure who was supposed to be my knight in shining armor. My hero, this time a female, just like in all the books I've read. But she didn't protect me in time before the ominous monster took over. I find myself disappointed that no one came to save me, and I am rattled that a dream has frightened me this much. It's been over a decade since nightmares have kept me awake like this.

Minutes pass and I am still not coming down from the shock and uneasiness. I can still feel the presence coming for me. I take a couple breaths before I decide to look at my phone to see what time it is. Coincidentally, three texts await me, meant to be one large message, all from Dad:

Ken: Why does it seem like you are starting an all-out war with us, and now including Grandpa in it? We aren't the devil, Katie. We are your parents. By the way the doctor said a bone in my back is broken and that I should take legal action. I'm unsure if I want to tell the cops that my daughter punched me in the back, but I may have no choice.

I read the words once again, my mouth agape in shock. He knows I've been in touch with Grandpa, maybe even that I had dinner with him tonight. Does that mean he knows I am staying here? It's possible that my heightened anxiety from my nightmare is still affecting me, but I shoot my eyes over to the bedroom door. It's 3:00 a.m., and not likely that he'll be here, but I scurry across the room and hastily lock the door again anyway. History has shown that this doesn't stop him from getting in, but I feel a bit calmer knowing he would at least be slowed down.

As I sit back down on the bed, I begin to think about his threat. His exaggerated claim that I 'punched him' and how he wants to turn me into the cops. Deep down, I know that his words are empty, especially since there is no way I broke the back of a man with about a hundred pounds on me when my palm was open. His message is a tactic he has used before and is only meant to scare me so I will back down. I may be able to logically assess that this is what he is doing, but the irrational part of my brain gives in to the fear and thinks about his persuasiveness. He knows how to use fear as a motivator for us to do as he wants. While I may realize the holes in his desperate ploy, not everyone else will. I don't even know if I will have the stamina to keep fighting him on this. Once he wants something, he never relents until he gets it.

He is trying to make me feel scared.

And it's working.

I now understand my dream. The danger surrounding me, drowning me as I gasp for air. *'I can keep you safe'*, the faceless 'hero' said as she was coming to save me. The one that never made it. Where is she now? Who is she?

Real life danger is lurking through the maze and I am trapped in the center alone.

I don't fall back asleep for the rest of the night.

CHAPTER 9

MARY:

I t is the middle of February, only one month since my mother died. My heart aches constantly for her, yet I cannot slow down to grieve since I have so many people pulling on me. My dad alone takes a vast amount of time each day as he is from a generation where the gender roles were concretely defined. I have found since my mom's passing that he does not understand the oven, microwave, dishwasher or other gadgets. He has no idea how to organize the household in terms of grocery lists, cleaning schedules, cooking and laundry. He has never been in charge of the social calendar or of his medical and other appointments. It's dawning on me quickly the responsibility of all this is now on my shoulders. And it's a heavy load to carry.

To alleviate some of my burden I have hired a lady named Sylvia, who cared for my mom before she died. She is kind and competent and an overall comfort to our entire family. She comes to my dad's house twice a week and makes a meal, cleans, does laundry, and pays attention to my father. She is a bright spot in a very difficult time and I couldn't be more pleased with having her help. This is why I am beyond crushed when I receive a surprising text while at the Loft from one of my closest friends who referred me to Sylvia.

Mary, call me asap. It's about Sylvia and Ken.

The familiar thud makes itself known in my chest whenever I hear his name.

"What's going on?" I say immediately into the call without even a hello.

"Sylvia says she cannot go back to your dad's house if Ken is there at the same time." My friend sounds upset.

"What happened?" I ask fearfully.

"I don't know all of it, but he scared her and did some inappropriate things. She is afraid to bring it up to you so she asked if I would."

I thank my friend and end the call.

Shit. Usually Ken does his worst damage inside the nucleus of our family. He seldom reveals his true deranged self to others because they do not tolerate it like we do. But this time he broke convention. Closing my eyes to temporarily block out what I have to do next, I massage my now pounding temples.

Taking a deep breath, I dial Sylvia's number and listen to the rings and my thumping chest like they are singing a duet. As soon as Sylvia answers my heart melts. She is so cute with her soft voice and semi-thick Spanish accent. When I am around her, I feel like everything will be just fine. She is a tough lady with an abusive past that she escaped more than two decades ago. The last thing she needs is to be around Ken.

I focus my attention on her as she begins sharing in her limited and broken English.

"I was vacuuming at your dad's house by myself. I did not hear anything until I backed into someone. I was so scared that I screamed and jumped away and turned around. I thought his face was familiar but couldn't tell for sure in his winter coat and hat. And then he spoke, and I knew it was Ken because his voice scares me. He said to me, 'Where is my dad?' That's all, no nothing like hello. He just stared at me with dark eyes. I tell him that they will be back soon, hoping this is true. My voice was shaking and he laughed at me. So quickly I moved to another room to keep working. A little while later I went to the bathroom to clean it. The door was wide open so I think it's empty, but Ken was standing in front of the toilet going to the bathroom. When he saw me he smiled in a weird way but keeps going. I saw his private parts. I tried to back away but then he turned and showed me everything while he slowly pulled up his pants. He just stood there with a smirk. He wanted me to see what I saw."

Vomit surfaces in my throat. I go to the kitchen, gulp some water, and force it back down.

"Your dad and Stuart came home just then. I did not want to say anything to them with Ken there, so I just tried to get my work done so I could leave. But behind your dad's back, Ken ordered me to get a spot out of his shirt. I was too afraid to say no. Then he asked me to help him button it up because he said he couldn't work buttons—something to do with his hands? He never took off his gloves. So I helped him, but I did not like to be that close to him and he scared me like my first husband. I do not want to quit, because I care for your dad, but I cannot be there if he is there."

My head is screaming, my ears hurt, my stomach is upside down.

"I'm so sorry, Sylvia," I barely choke out the insufficient words. "I assure you, he will never be there with you again. You have my word." She seems embarrassed but thanks me anyway before we hang up.

Running into the bathroom, I throw up in the toilet, screaming in disgust practically at the same time. Thank goodness I'm alone here at the Loft and the front door is locked.

Those damn hands are his excuse for everything now. Ever since the accident he uses them to get more attention and do even less for himself, which I didn't think was possible. He talks about them all the time, as if he's the only one who has ever experienced pain. And he plays the victim, conveniently avoiding the fact that he caused the accident himself, six years ago this very month.

*****

I hate February in Illinois. It's grey and cold and raw for most of the month. There is an ominous feeling to each day like we are never going to see the sun again and that something bad is looming. 2009 has started out worse than ever so it's not shocking to find myself in the ER with a bowel obstruction. My intestinal problems since birth have evolved into multiple surgeries leading to scar tissue formation. When this scar tissue blocks my digestion, everything backs up. It is the worst pain I have ever experienced, and mothers who have had it say it's worse than labor. It is like being stabbed repeatedly with a butcher knife and this is one is one of the worst of the worsts. If a nasal-gastric (NG) tube doesn't fix it, it means more surgery because eventually the intestines will burst and kill you. The NG tube sucks all the food in your system out of your nose with the hope of relieving some pressure so things can shift and perhaps self-correct.

Terry is with me in the hospital room as I have now been admitted. I ask him to call my parents since we are supposed to get together the following day. When I see my mom calling, I assume it's because she is worried about me.

"Hi, Mom."

"Mary, it's bad."

"I know, but it will be okay." I'm touched she is so concerned.

"It's about Ken. Ken is bad," she clarifies.

I am tempted to hang up. Are we seriously going to talk about Ken when I am in complete misery?

"What's happening, Mom?" I ask with the most compassion I can muster.

"Ken is in the hospital with severe frostbite. He passed out in the snow overnight. He may have to have his hands am . . . pu . . . tated." That last word gets lost in her throat.

"Surely, Ken is exaggerating, Mom." He can take a hangnail and turn it into this.

"No, Mary, I talked to June. She is hysterical. His hands are completely black according to her."

I try to obscure the sounds from a large tube coming out of my nose and food passing through it. Apparently, my mom does not even know I'm in the hospital, or her hysteria has caused her to forget.

"June said that Ken got fired from his coaching job last night. He left the house in a rage and as of this morning was not back."

There is a pause and I hear my mom blowing her nose. Surely, she has been crying which is rare these days for her. Ever since she went through menopause, she says it takes a lot for her to produce any tears.

"Somebody ended up finding Ken about 7:00 this morning. He was passed out in a snowbank. He did not have gloves on. June thinks he was there for hours since the bars close at 2:00 a.m."

Another pause. I hear her gulping fluid. My head starts to pound. It has been as cold of a February as they come, right now in the early afternoon just about zero without the wind chill. We have been digging out from record amounts of snow since November. Five hours? Overnight? No gloves?

"He's in intensive care up in Milwaukee. His blood alcohol level was over three times the legal limit. Dad and I are leaving now to go up there. He might lose his hands, Mary." She begins to sob uncontrollably.

Even with a tube coming out of my nose and my throat feeling like I've swallowed razor blades, I normally would have something to say that would make the situation less bad. I've got nothing.

"Keep me posted, Mom. I love you," is all I can think of.

Any attention to my discomfort is now drowned out by my spinning thoughts. Maybe this will be good. Maybe Ken will stop drinking or even go to rehab. Maybe everyone in our family will come together and at last admit that he needs help. They say everyone has a bottom, a time where it hits even the hardest of addicts that they have had enough. That even they are ready to change. This has to be Ken's, right? How can it possibly get worse?

*****

The doctors put Ken in hyperbaric chambers on and off for a month, breathing pure oxygen into a pressurized room up to three times the normal air pressure. Under these conditions your lungs gather more oxygen than is normally possible, allowing your blood to carry it throughout your body and promote healing. They said Ken had incredible blood flow. They even wrote him up in a medical journal. His hands, which had lost all skin and nails and swelled like sausages, healed completely, with the exception of a few scars. They called Ken a medical miracle.

I had major surgery that same weekend. My health issues and multiple surgeries have resulted in a chronic intestinal bleed that cannot be fixed.

Ken has incredible blood flow. I don't have enough blood. Ken abuses his body. I take care of myself but am sick. Ken is a medical miracle. I now get blood transfusions to stay alive.

Where is my medical miracle?

I kneel here in front of the toilet, unable to move from the repugnance that is Ken. The word 'unfair' seems pathetically weak as a description of my life compared to his, of my place in the family as the lowly servant and him the royal king. I cannot and will not let him ruin my chance of having Sylvia help me. Exposing himself has got to be even too much for my dad to ignore, right? His path of destruction must end, and Katie and I are trying to figure out how to make that happen.

CHAPTER 10

KATIE:

*S*leep, eat, pack up, and leave. That has been my routine these past couple weeks at the Libertyville house. Now that Dad knows I have been communicating with Grandpa, he has made it his mission to come to Libertyville every weekend. I don't dare leave anything out in the guest bedroom, nor do I allow it to be in any condition except its original polished state. I have been desperate to stay away from him, especially now that he is threatening to call the cops on me. I know I will never convince him to leave me alone about his back, so I don't even try. I know the truth and, even as upset as I was, there was no way I broke his back from slapping him.

I confessed to Mary what happened because I was so scared, not of his back actually being broken, but that he could somehow trick people into thinking that it was. I didn't even feel comfortable telling her about it, since it makes me look like a violent person, but I had to admit it out loud to someone. She told me that my dad can bring out the worst in all of us and invoke responses that we wouldn't have otherwise. She insisted that I am not a bad person when another person constantly instigates the ugly out of people, and that helped me ease my worry.

It doesn't, however, make my living situation any easier. Grandpa continues to let me stay at his house even though it is causing a divide in the family. I've been there only a few weeks and I am still adjusting to these people and this life. I am terrified of Grandpa kicking me out so am careful of the things I say and do. So far, he has shown no indication of doing such a thing. Mary seems to think having someone young around takes away from the gloomy atmosphere left behind from Grandma's death. I hope she is right and that I am not as much of a burden as I feel I am. I would go live with Mary and Terry in their adorable farmhouse just ten minutes north of here, but they have a dog, Dixie, that will supposedly 'eat my face' as Mary says. The dog doesn't like strangers. Because of this, we decided mutually not to even try it.

The search for full-time work has become a daunting task. I've sent out countless resumes, with no luck in return. Fortunately, I was able to pick up a part-time gig as a receptionist at a chiropractic office in downtown Libertyville and have been spending five or six hours a day there. In the meantime, Mary's clients have been offering me dog-sitting roles to add a little extra cash flow as I plan how to make a full-time living. The list of ways I am indebted to Mary keeps growing by the day. One of Mary's clients, Lorrie, is currently letting me stay at her place to watch her dog, Callie. It works out great because I don't have to pack up my stuff for an entire week. This house is off Dad's radar even if it is only a mile away from Grandpa's. I want to make a good impression on her—gratitude doesn't even begin to cover how I feel that someone is helping me at all.

I sit down on the couch in Lorrie's home with Callie at my feet. The house is beautiful and has a homey feel to it even though it is quite spacious. From the cedar floors to the high ceilings and plush furniture, I find myself very comfortable with my stay here the past couple of days. After the film I am watching wraps up, I remember I still have to take Callie out one last time before bed.

Lorrie has a fenced in backyard but prefers Callie to go out the front on a leash because she has a tendency to eat sticks when not watched properly. I grab her leash and harness and take a few minutes to coax her over to me so I can put it on. My jacket, a thin outer lining of a ski jacket, slips over my shoulders and I quickly slide on my pair of black dress flats that I wore earlier today since I'm too lazy to put on winter shoes. It is cold outside with snow on the ground, but I'll only be out for a minute or two, so it should be alright. As I open the front door, I am immediately hit with a blast of air that numbs my nose. I hope this dog does her business fast so I can escape back into the warmth as soon as possible. As we finally break through the doorway, Callie starts to move towards the designated patch of shoveled grass and I reflexively reach around and close the door behind me.

The second it latches, I halt in my tracks. I feel in my pockets for the garage opener that Lorrie gave me to open the house, but my hands come up empty. I then remember the exact spot I left it on the counter next to my car keys and my phone.

I drag Callie around the house to see if there is a door somewhere that by chance is open. Unfortunately, though, I had just gone around and locked everything as part of my nightly routine. Being someone who watched far too many horror movies as a kid, I have learned to thoroughly secure myself in at night. I close my eyes in frustration at myself and take a deep breath to calm down so I can figure out what to do next. I have no way to get in the house, no keys to my car in the driveway, and no phone to call anyone. I only have one option.

Walk to Grandpa's house.

As the rest of my face begins to numb, I don't waste another second and start pulling Callie in the direction of Grandpa's. It must be close to midnight at this point, so I am hoping that someone will miraculously be awake there. The latest those two go to bed is 9:00 or 10:00 on a 'crazy night.'

I try to think of anything else besides the painfully exposed skin on the top of my feet, as I walk as fast as can through the night. For some reason, I try talking to Callie as if to calm down a scared child. *We're almost there, Callie. Keep going, you're doing good!* In reality, though, she probably just thinks we are out for a late night walk without a care in the world. How I wish I had the mindset of a dog sometimes.

The fastest way to get to Grandpa's house is to go over a bridge that crosses an inlet of a small lake, with a wooded area surrounding it. I can either go the long way in the well-lit suburban neighborhoods, or through this much quicker, but dark and scary path in which there is sure to be a criminal. As numbness tingles at my fingers, I remember Dad's accident and feel panic cloud its way into my chest at the thought of getting frostbite on my uncovered hands. It propels me through the wooded shortcut littered with potential murderers in my mind and mentally prepares me to fight anyone that dares to cross me or this dog. The thought alone makes me laugh, alleviating the fear for a split second.

I get to my destination a few minutes later. When I walk up the front steps, I am delighted to find the front door unlocked as I reach for it. I relish the heat washing over me as Callie and I step inside. This place feels like a sanctuary compared to the cold walk over here.

Taking a seat in the kitchen for a few minutes to let my fingers and toes thaw out a bit, I think about calling Mary. I am so ashamed. She has been so kind to me this past month, and I feel like doing something stupid like this would let her down. Regardless of how late it is, I end up dialing her number.

She answers on the first ring, which surprises me. She is another one in this family who goes to bed early. She has told me her nightly routine is to drink her wine all evening as she cares for Grandpa, then stagger home about 10:00 p.m. and pass out immediately in the living room recliner. I wonder if I should be worried about her drinking behavior, but then push that thought aside as I have too much to deal with right now.

I apologize for messing up this job opportunity so soon, but Mary seems understanding about the whole thing, saying she will sort it out with Lorrie in the morning. In the meantime, we agree I'll stay here at Grandpa's house with the dog. I let embarrassment wash over me despite Mary's patient acceptance.

After hanging up, exhaustion swallows me and I long to go to bed. Looking for Callie, who was on the other side of the kitchen island a minute ago, I realize she is no longer there. I exit the room and peer into the living room on the other side of the door. No dog. I quickly search the downstairs family room, and even the basement, while calling out her name as quietly as I can. I don't want to wake the sleeping members of this house, especially when they don't know I'm here. I grow increasingly frustrated by the lack of the brown fur-ball walking around as I think I have now searched the whole house.

I head upstairs as a last-ditch effort to find her and notice that Grandpa's door is cracked open, uncharacteristic for him. My heart races as I tiptoe up to it, hoping it doesn't mean what I think it does. Slowly pushing open the door, I glance into the dark room. As my eyes adjust, I see Grandpa's figure under the blanket, sleeping soundly on his side. Just past him, but also on the bed, is the silhouette of Callie standing tall on all fours. Her ears are perked up as she stares back at me. I can tell she is mocking me, ready to play. My heart rate jackhammers but at the same time, I stifle a laugh.

"Callie, come!" I hiss urgently as my heart barrels itself in my chest. She doesn't budge, and I can tell this is a game to her. I quietly take a step further into the room to get her. Inches from the bed, Grandpa rolls over and stares at me, seeming to wake finally from my presence.

"I'm so sorry, she just came in here and I had no idea," I immediately blabber as I gesture at Callie standing next to his horizontal body on the bed.

He sees Callie for what appears to be the first time, then rolls back over without another word, as if it is the most normal thing in the world for a random dog to be on his bed, and for his granddaughter, who was supposed to be gone, to be in his room at midnight. I chase Callie out of the room and quickly bring her into mine across the hall.

We reach my bed and Callie climbs up and lies at my feet. As soon as we are both situated and I know we are out of earshot of Grandpa, I let out the laugh that I had been holding in. I don't know if it is from the stress of this evening, exhaustion, or how goofy Callie looked on Grandpa's bed, but the laughter feels good. I know I'll have to explain this later, and I have no idea how everyone is going to respond, but in the moment, I don't care. Callie stares at me blankly and there is a part of me that wishes she could see the humor in this situation, too, so the two of us could laugh together.

CHAPTER 11

MARY:

My mind is mush. I cannot catch a breath, and time to mourn for my mom does not exist. My dad needs my attention constantly, Stuart calls several times a day, my business is suffering due to neglect, and I barely see my husband or friends. My days start at 6:00 a.m. and do not stop until collapsing into bed after 10:00 p.m. The clock ticks loudly no matter where I am, reminding me that I am due at the next location soon. There is no fun to be had since it is all obligations and chores at each place. There is never enough time to be effective and I am regularly disappointing someone because I am late, or cannot stay long, or do not accomplish what was promised. What happened to getting balance back in my life?

As for Katie, the dichotomy of her delightful personality coupled with being Ken's child is tough to reconcile. Our relationship consumes time I don't have as she sorts through her feelings about her childhood. This comes with a mental cost that is beating me down, twisting me up, and sending me back to the edge of insanity. I am having a hard time differentiating between her abuse and mine as the stories that surface are so frighteningly similar, I can barely listen. Hopefully not everything is similar, but I'm afraid to ask.

Ironically, in the most cutting of ways, all the players in Ken's family equate to the ones in mine. June is my dad, always working to make the money, calm and detached at home. Sandra is my mom, the one who defers to God and forgiveness as if this cannot coexist with 'tough-love'. Josh is Stuart, neutral as much as possible, yet very aware of the dynamics. Obviously, Ken is himself, but this too is disturbing in that NOTHING has changed with his illness in all this time. Katie is me, the voice, the chosen one to stand up for what is right and, therefore, banished for breaking the family decree of 'keeping the peace'. When I look at Katie, I see my own suffering reflected in her eyes.

Terry wants me to distance myself from Katie, saying I do not need the tension that comes from Ken by being her confidante and friend. It took decades to rebuild myself into someone other than Ken's victim and within only a few weeks I have lost much of that strength. Ken is circling, I can feel him, he is invading my brain like a virus. Yet every time Katie pops up on a call or in person, my heart is full and everything seems right. I wish I would have had a 'me' when I was her age. How can I turn her away?

Today is a Pilates, Weights, Cardio class at my business. This type of workout requires upbeat and energetic music, and Katie has made it her mission to introduce me to the band *One Direction*. She is a huge fan; emphasizing that the word *fan* comes from *fanatic*, which I believe she is in the most amusing of ways. We are just starting the Cardio portion of the class when "Best Song Ever" comes on and Katie launches into a concert dance, throwing her arms up at various intervals. I find myself joining her. We both start singing along at the same time.

"Clearly you two are related!" my peeps exclaim as they once again show how they have embraced Katie as part of the Fitness Loft family.

After class, when everyone else has left, Katie and I plop on the stage in our usual spots, immediately launching into our fluid conversation that has become the recent norm. I'm continually impressed with Katie's openness, strength, and sense of what is real. This is unknown territory in our family and often seems too good to be true. My thoughts regularly imagine the time when she will surely revert to the doctrine of denial and I will once again be alone in exile.

"I can't believe my dad did that to Sylvia." Katie gets that look of despair I've now come to recognize in her body language. "Just when I think he can't disgust me more, he goes down another level".

"I know, sweetie. It's really sick. I can't imagine being his daughter."

"I can't imagine being his sister."

There is a comfortable silence between us that comes from being understood. Sometimes no more words need to be said.

KATIE:

As I sit on the stage with Mary, my mind reflects on everything she and I just talked about. I think about poor Sylvia being forced to see the nudity of my father. The thought alone repulses me, especially since she is such a sweet woman. I try to talk to her every week when she comes to Grandpa's house and feel like I already know so much about her life. Dad, on the other hand, is not sweet. I am reminded of all the embarrassment I have felt whenever he would drunkenly hit on a waitress in front of all of us, including Mom. I was beyond ashamed to be sitting at the same table, somehow connected to this sleazy man with a continuous sheen of sweat across his forehead. Mary and I have confessed to each other that we both have felt uncomfortable with how he acted with us, typically wishing to escape his too-long hugs and possessive attitude. Mary calls it mental rape. I have never heard anyone say something like that and now am trying to wrap my head around it. But she is right, even if those particular words are hard to take. To rape is to control, and Dad always wanted control over us.

A week has now passed since the dog-sitting incident, and Mary and Lorrie were surprisingly cool about the whole thing, even teasing me in class. I'm glad we could laugh together and that I haven't broken Mary's new trust in me.

"Did you hear my dad's latest claim?" I ask Mary. She shakes her head no.

"Well, I had lunch with my mom a couple days ago, and apparently he told her that he was working for the cops when he was ordering Percocet."

Mary laughs. "Seriously?"

I wonder if this was the story he was going to use during the 'family meeting" he wanted me to attend a few weeks back. Or maybe he just came up with this new spin. "He couldn't offer any proof though, saying it was too dangerous," I continue.

She rolls her eyes. "Of course, he would say that."

Having lunch with Mom was the first time I saw her since I left the house. The conversation was awkward, but it was worth it to show that I still want a relationship with her even when taking space from Dad. Mary told me that she and Grandma *agreed to disagree* about the problems Dad brought them throughout the years. If they were able remain close, then surely Mom and I can, too. I don't believe for one second that he was working for the cops. When Mom thought it over, she told me she was proud of me for standing up to him.

"At least my mom and I can still talk to each other. Just like you and Grandma," I share with Mary.

"That's so great, sweetie, even if Ken is a nutcase." Mary rolls her eyes.

I chuckle in response and get ready to head out. I always feel lighter after one of Mary's classes. She shares stories that take place in our lives while teaching on stage. Mary's peeps always laugh at the situations we get ourselves into, from things like the dog-sitting incident to something outrageous that Dad did. Any client who attends Mary's class will be completely in-the-loop on the saga that is my family. There is no judgement with them, though—they comment only in empathy. I'm learning that all of the hardships of life can always be turned into humor if you know how to look for it.

I laugh along with the peeps, most of the time genuinely. For me, telling a story has always made it seem easy to pretend that the abuse wasn't a big deal. Making people smile is a way to frame it in a way that brushes it off as nothing, and I live for entertaining people.

My socialite status started in college. I always did crazy things just to get reactions out of people. They called me fun, hilarious, and full of life. I loved it. I *craved* it. I even believed it about myself most of the time. *See, Dad? See how well-liked I am? I am not a bad person like you think I am.* I swear I would repeat this in my head to him over and over again just to prove it to myself. But the people who put on the biggest show on the grand stage of life typically are the ones with the most to hide behind the curtain.

All it takes is one call from him or even just seeing his name flash across my phone screen and this 'cheerful person' turns into anything but. I try to convince myself that I can be strong enough to be around him again someday, but only with more time apart. To the outside world, they see my life by adding up the happy moments, but never subtracting the sad ones. When we talk in Mary's classes, I feel it again—that elation that comes with telling a story. A grand tale. But I am trapped under the weight pressing on my chest that reminds me that this actually isn't some tale for me like it is for them. This is my life.

I am happy. I am not.

CHAPTER 12

MARY:

Ken claims he doesn't drink anymore since the accident in the snow. But even if this is true, he pops pills all day long. He says his hands are on fire, or they itch until he cannot stand it, or they are so cold that he wears those dirty black gloves even in the middle of summer. He claims that he is taking the narcotics the prescribed way, following the doctor's orders. But he has become deranged. And Katie caught him ordering drugs off the streets. He knows she has proof and he's scared. The latest text shows just how desperate he is.

Ken: For the past six months I have had to do a lot of lying. I was not allowed to talk about the situation for safety sake. I hate dope dealers with a passion and I did something about it. I have been working for the FBI to get the drug lords off the street. Can you tell Katie this?

I laugh to myself because he told June it was the cops, not the FBI. He can't even keep his lies straight. I choose to taunt him.

Mary: Is part of the job actually taking the pills, Ken?

Ken: I don't know what you are talking about.

Mary: You are high all the time. I see the bottles.

Ken: It's part of the act, Mary. I am not complete scum.

Mary: What about last year? Was your overdose also part of the act?

*****

My phone rings in the distance but I don't get up. It's a beautiful September night and I am enjoying some peace in front of a small bonfire with Terry. I need this moment to soothe the worry that has come from my dad's emergency brain surgery. They seemed to have caught the hemorrhage in time. We will know for sure once he wakes up. I just left the hospital after eight excruciatingly long hours since they said he will sleep until tomorrow.

The phone rings again. Reluctantly I retrieve it and answer. It is Stuart, clearly panicked by the rapidity of his speech. I hit the speaker button so Terry can hear too.

"It's Ken. He's here barricading all the doors with furniture. He says the terrorists are out to get him. He told me to stay away from the windows. He has a knife and a baseball bat."

I look to Terry, who rolls his eyes in his ever-calm way of NOT reacting to Ken's drama. I, on the other hand, am flustered by this vision of Ken. Even he doesn't become this delusional often. Is he playing a game for attention or is he really tripping this time?

"Mom is still at the hospital?" I already know the answer.

"Correct. I'm terrified." Stuart's voice catches.

"Terry is going to call the police." I already see him pulling out his phone as he mouths those words to me.

"Are you sure that's a good idea? He will get mad," Stuart states as if that's anything new.

"He will get mad? He is barricading the door and pulling out weapons. I think he's already mad." Terry jumps in with logic that is never used by the Albrechts. He's on the phone with 911 before Stuart or I can say another word.

———

There are multiple blue and red lights in front of my parents' house when we turn onto their street. We are confronted by a police officer for ID and allowed to enter. The scene in front of me is disturbing. Furniture is overturned, doors are blocked, blinds are drawn. Stuart's car is gone so he must have gotten away. All the rooms are black except where Ken sits in the living room, surrounded by paramedics, medical equipment, and at least a dozen prescription pill bottles scattered across the coffee table.

Ken is babbling. "I have to get back to my horses! Don't you know who I am?! I'm an international horse trainer and my horses are waiting for me. Get these tubes out of me! I have to get back to my horses!"

A paramedic glances over at me, catching my eye with a look of bewilderment. I shake my head, remaining out of view of Ken, letting the paramedic know that Ken is most definitely NOT an international horse trainer. Terry smirks.

"It's really in your best interest to go get checked out at the hospital, sir. Your vitals show that you have clearly overdosed." Another EMT is trying to reason with this madman that is my brother.

"NOOOOOO, I am NOT going to the hospital! I need to get to my horses. Why don't you underst . . . "

He passes out and they load him into the ambulance.

———

Approaching the front desk at the emergency room, Terry and I hear sounds like a wild animal in horrible pain. It doesn't take long to figure out it is Ken.

"Get me the fuck out of here! You have no right to keep me. I will sue you all. I am a wealthy attorney that can take you all down."

I peek around the curtain. He is strapped down, his body convulsing against the restraints, his face warped with anger. This HAS to be enough to send him to a mental hospital and finally get the help he needs. However, I am shocked by the callousness of the doctor when he tells me that mental health decisions are not in their power. Once Ken becomes medically stable, he will be released.

"Let me get this straight... he overdoses, is delusional, needs restraints, and is screaming loud enough to hear from the street... and a mental health evaluation isn't warranted?" I'm losing my cool, I can hear it in my shrill voice.

"That's correct, ma'am. He has to consent to a mental health check-up." The doctor may as well be a robot speaking, his eyes and inflection are that lifeless.

"But he's not mentally well enough to know better!" My husband tugs on my arm, encouraging me to leave it be.

The doctor turns to walk away, muttering something about the system and how it works.

*****

They released Ken at 3:00 a.m., just a few hours later. They even called him a cab.

Snapping back from the memory, I continue the text exchange with Ken, reminding him of this ludicrous overdose episode just a few years ago.

Ken: YOU made up the horse trainer story Mary! You are always out to get me.

Mary: How could I make up paramedics and the hospital?

Ken: You called an ambulance for no reason just to stick it to me.

Mary: But they wouldn't have taken you in if there wasn't a reason, Ken.

Ken: BULLSHIT! That's all you EVER have in your lying mind. STOP with the non-truths or I will be forced to use my FBI ties to take you down.

Turning off my phone, I pull out a beer, pop it open, and guzzle over half of it down. I'm not even sure why I continue to engage with this deranged beast, except that maybe it feels good to no longer be afraid of the biting disdain that would always come from my mom when I used to do it before. As the weeks roll on with Katie around, I am finding it nearly impossible to continue the family dictum of looking the other way. Speaking the truth, whether heard or not by others, is becoming rewarding enough. It is killing Ken to have Katie exposing his vile to his number one enemy—me. I can see he is becoming more unhinged than ever. Interesting that the more insanity he reveals, the more lucid I feel around it for the first time in my life. My sense of right and wrong is getting untangled from the distortion of my mom's messages and fear of revenge from Ken.

I have spent a lot of time thinking about the general concept of poor mental health. I've studied it, talked through it, written about it, lived it. Yet it remains a mystery as to how to cure it. Especially how to cure Ken. People say things like 'My brother is an alcoholic too' and 'We have depression in our family as well' . . . trying to relate to my stories of Ken. But unless you know him closely, it is impossible to convey the depths of his mental distortion. You could take the most depressed, narcissistic, addicted, manipulative, angry, paranoid, dishonest sociopath and multiply the force by 100 and still not get to the core of who Ken is. Sandra once said he needs his own entry in the dictionary because no current words come remotely close to describing him. He is frighteningly unique. An enigma.

How can anyone with mental illness ever get better if part of the illness is that they don't want to? But perhaps they don't want to because the disease is working for them somehow? Certainly, when our family dances around Ken and lets him have his way—even giving him extraordinary amounts of money in my parents' case—it rewards the behavior enough to keep it going. But is it that simple? Would the typical 'Tough Love' work for someone so atypical, almost non-human? I struggle with answers, though

I always acted so sure when I argued with my mom. Ultimately, I was hoping that we would try something different, since the family system, as it stood, wasn't helping him or us. Not making things worse does not equate to making things better. It's important to do things just because they are right regardless of the outcome. 'Turning the other cheek', 'sweeping it under the rug' was most assuredly wrong on so many levels. If standing up to him made it worse temporarily, or even permanently, it would have been worth it knowing we did it to be real, to be truthful, to be strong. My mom couldn't or wouldn't see that, but maybe now the rest of us can.

CHAPTER 13

KATIE:

There is a soft melody in the distance. Stuart must be playing the piano again. According to both him and Mary, he was never taught by anyone how to do it; the gift just came out one day. The music he produces is genius in every sense of the word. What is truly amazing is that he never plays the same thing twice. They are unique tunes within his head, all extraordinarily beautiful.

During the last month of living here, I have learned so much about this side of the family. We have been going out to eat several times a week, which would seem like we are doing it to have fun, but the reality is that none of us knows how to cook. During one of these outings, I finally built up enough courage to ask Stuart why he talks to himself. It has been something my siblings and I have wondered about for years, and I am sick of sweeping it away and out of sight just like every other problem in our family.

I was shocked that Stuart wasn't upset with my question. Quite the opposite, it was a very light-hearted conversation. He admitted that he doesn't usually know he's saying things out loud but explains that he is rehearsing a conversation with someone who is real but isn't there at the moment. It's his way of sorting out what he wishes he would say to them in person. Most of the time he is 'speaking' to my dad after he has done something terrible.

I also learned that Mary has owned a house in Lake Geneva, Wisconsin for almost a decade and has miraculously been able to keep that information away from Dad. If he knew, he would surely be obsessively jealous and would badger her to go there. But since it is off the grid, Mary offered it to me as place to live and hide. It means the world that she trusts me with her secret and that she knows how serious I am about staying away from Dad. It makes me sad that she has to hide something like a vacation home from everyone because she cannot let her older brother know. I wonder how much she, and everyone else in the family, has been hiding.

Living in Mary's Lake Geneva home sounds nice, but I am not sure I want to be *that* isolated from everyone. It's enjoyable being with relatives that I don't have to tiptoe around because I'm waiting for their fragile shell to crack. It's not easy living here, though. Dad is calling and texting me almost every single day since he found out. They are hateful messages, so I have put him on my spam list. He still claims he's working for the cops, and now the FBI according to Mary, but the more excuses he gives, the less I believe him. I'm trying to sift through the ocean of lies when I all I want is a splash of truth.

My birthday is this Tuesday, March 3rd. I don't have any plans, but I know I don't want to spend it with Dad. According to Mary, he has already been getting on her case for it. As my curiosity piques, I open up my auto-reject list and see his name flash across the screen. I would like to say that I ignore his voicemails and messages, but something always lures me back to them. I find myself hoping that maybe he is finally calling to open up about all of his secrets and take responsibility for his lies and abuse. I press 'play' and the first sound that comes through the receiver is an angry sigh.

"Katie, your mother wants to have a birthday party for you here at our house." Another sigh. "But that is only if we can get ahold of you first." A grunt-like breath now. "It would be nice if you called us back for once instead of thinking of yourself and ignoring us. It would mean a lot to your mother. She would really like to celebrate your birthday with you." *Click.*

I feel disappointment spread through me as I set my phone down. I crave for him to be able to hear how much pain cries from my heart whenever I have confronted him over the years. I have been hoping that my rejection would make him try to be nicer and to get help. If a daughter that you claim to love won't talk to you, wouldn't you want to change?

Reality checks in as I bury those emotions, something I have done many times in my life. Maybe he isn't capable of loving me the way I want to be loved, or maybe it's that there isn't real love at all. Love is more than saying the words after all. It's a verb, an action. You show people you love them by respecting them, trusting them, enjoying their company. At least Mom knows that I am not avoiding her specifically. I have told her this a lot.

I let these thoughts settle within my mind as I get ready for yoga class. Since I am already late, I scurry around my room to get dressed and make my way over to the Loft. I don't see Grandpa or Stuart when I leave so I walk out without saying goodbye. Even though I arrive about seven minutes late, Mary is just stepping onto the podium to begin class. Her internal clock runs later than most people, another thing we have in common. I move through the poses and tune out as the peeps talk about their lives. The class flies by and everyone clears out, leaving Mary and I to talk on the stage, as has become our norm. We discuss the birthday party my parents are throwing for me in Wisconsin. Even though they know I am not going, apparently Grandpa and Stuart are planning on attending it. I am saddened that the people I'm living with would openly choose to spend my birthday with my problematic father and not with me.

"Could we maybe do something for my birthday?" I ask Mary with trepidation.

"Certainly—if that's what *you* want," Mary responds with emphasis on *you*.

"Yeah, I mean, it doesn't have to be a big thing or anything like that. Maybe we could just grab dinner with a few folks?" I hate myself for sounding so insecure. I always worry that I am asking for too much.

"Yes, of course we can do that, sweetie. I just didn't know if that was something that you wanted or not," Mary reiterates.

"I didn't either, to be honest, but now I think it would be nice to spend time with some of the people I've met since moving here. They have become important to me." I didn't realize how much so until just now.

"I can see if some of the peeps would like to come, but I don't know about Stuart and Grandpa. They seem to want to go up to see your parents, even though it's *your* birthday." Mary sighs in disbelief.

"That's fine," I pause. "I can't stop them, it's just kind of sad that my dad would try to pull away the people I am living with on my birthday when I am not going to be there. But I think it would be great if some peeps came—maybe Sylvia, too?"

As I think of people I can invite in the area, I realize that not one of them is even close to my age. With a thud to my brain it dawns on me how drastically my life has changed in just a few months, especially since leaving college.

"Great, I will see who I can round up then!" Mary is always so positive. Refreshing compared to who I grew up with, meaning Dad.

I wish I could invite Mom, but unfortunately, I don't trust that she will withhold information from Dad. Time and time again, she has disappointed me by doing quite the opposite. This party with Mary would be nice, though. I really love how close we have gotten in just a short time. Even if my parents don't want me to spend it with Mary, I don't care. Why is *my* birthday more about them than me?

Chapter 14

Katie:

I hear my phone buzz and my eyes fly open. Darkness surrounds me in the bedroom at Grandpa's house. I look towards the light to try to see who is calling me at 7:00 in the morning. Instead of calls, I see texts, Facebook posts, and Snapchats littering my screen. After letting my eyes adjust to the harsh brightness, I look at the date. *March 3.* While still in my groggy half-asleep state, I put together what these notifications are for. Today is my 23rd birthday.

It's only a few hours into my special day, and people I love are already making me feel on top of the world. There is a warmth that is spreading to my chest, and it gives me hope. If these people love me, maybe I am not as selfish as Dad seems to think I am. I quickly sift through the messages, and my heart stills as my eyes land on one in particular. I anxiously open it, not knowing what to expect. I gasp as I read it:

Mom: Happy birthday Katie! While you are celebrating today, just remember the two people who brought you into this world, you want absolutely nothing to do with.

I freeze as I try to process the message. That doesn't sound like Mom's words. Did Dad write it from her phone? Or maybe it actually *was* her? How she could think I want nothing to do with her is baffling since I have always told her exactly the opposite. She recently said she understood why I am keeping my distance. I thought she got how bad this is.

It's like the elation from all the other messages is just thrown out the window, fluttering into the cold March wind. Any gratification wipes itself clean when the one person who matters most is offering cruelties instead of love and support.

Robotically, I get ready to go to the Loft, but I am numb. Maybe I will call Mary and tell her I'm not up to it. But I really don't want Dad to be the cause of me wallowing, not today of all days. Then he takes even more from me. Or is it now 'they'? If I leave now, maybe I can talk to Mary before class—this message from my mom unsettles me too much to keep inside.

MARY:

#%@/>#%\@ calling...

Otherwise known as Ken.

I long ago made this his contact name because it puts him at the bottom of the list. It's funny, too, since he doesn't know I've done this . . . a small victory for my lifetime of squelched rights. I let it go to voicemail because next will come his texts—now coined 'torture texts' by Katie and me. When asked why he isn't blocked, I tell people it's better to know what latest delusion engulfs his brain for self-protection. And at least this way I am not sickened by his ugly voice.

Ken: I know you think of yourself as a decent person. Well a decent person would have realized by now the enormous toll Katie's behavior has taken on her mother and tried to stop it. You are enabling the situation by not trying to get Katie to talk to us. Stop lying. Would a decent person seem to like a part of the family being destroyed? Or would a decent person put her foot down with Katie and stick up for her mom for once. Katie's mom is the woman who gave her life, a person who has deserved absolutely none of this. Which would a decent person do Mary? Do you care at all? Or is it that you want to be Katie's pretend mom? Hard to tell with you. You have so many damn secrets most of which I know about. All safely stored away though organized and for use when the time comes.

Pain sears across my face and into my ears as I grind my teeth.

Ken: If you could just get Katie to meet us somewhere to talk this out then I will admit to myself THAT MARY IS A DECENT PERSON AFTER ALL. PLEASE TRY FOR YOUR SISTER-IN-LAW'S SAKE. SHE IS FEELING THAT NEITHER OF US IS WELCOME IN THAT FAMILY ANYMORE. IS THAT TRUE? We want to speak with Katie privately but if she needs moral support why don't you come too? Maybe just excuse yourself for 10-15 minutes so we could ask Katie a couple of questions alone. This is really important because time is not our friend. Please Mary not only for me but especially for June, and Katie long-term as well … please make this happen. This is your big brother reaching out to you. A part of me still loves my sister. Prove to me that you are deserving of that. You really don't want June and Katie to lose forever that special mother-daughter relationship that has existed for well over two decades do you Mary? You can do this I know you can.

Rolling my head in an attempt to get my neck to loosen, I notice my shoulders are practically up at my ears. Disgust swallows me up from seeing the words 'big brother' and 'loves my sister' in back to back sentences, as if he has any right to such closeness with me. That familiar feeling of mental rape consumes my senses.

My spinning thoughts are interrupted by the sound of the bells and the front door opening. I enjoy my daily game of guessing who might be the first customer to arrive at the Loft as I hear each footstep on the stairs. However, these sounds are unfamiliar and heavy, and I am surprised when I see it's Katie. Usually she bounds up the stairs full of energy, and since today is her birthday, I would expect it even more.

"Happy birthd…" I start to proclaim, freezing upon noticing Katie's blotchy face and swollen eyes. Tension instantly penetrates the room. This has to be about Ken.

"I just got a cruel text from my mom." Katie's voice is barely discernible.

"From your *mom*?" Surely, I heard wrong.

"Yes, my mom sent this."

Mom: Just remember that the two people that brought you into this world are the two people you want absolutely nothing to do with.

"That has to be your dad using her phone." I'm certain this is the case after reading the text message.

"I originally thought that, but she said she was at work already."

"No *I love you*?" This isn't the June I know.

"Nope."

"I thought she was proud of you for getting out."

"Not anymore." Katie shakes with grief.

He got to her.

"I'm sure she will come to her senses, Katie. Besides, you made it clear it wasn't her you are running from."

Katie nods as we get interrupted by customers coming in for class.

I've always wished that the Ken factor wasn't a monumental deterrent to being closer to June, like sisters. She has a calm, pleasant way of conversing, and she is interested in all of us. She is stable, capable, and has done wonders with their children because, despite what I know took place, they are all three fantastic people. She downplays the distortion of Ken, which I guess can be considered a detriment, but we have all said at one time or another that she is a saint to minimize how much damage he could really do if he were around us more. Especially now that he is so sick and disabled, how would he ever support himself without her? I shudder at the thought of him living in Libertyville once again. I'm convinced of June's good character and am sure that she understands why Katie is doing what she needs to do for her own mental well-being. Surely, maternal instinct is stronger than Ken's manipulative pull.

———

Later, after Katie has left, I see June's name pop up on the phone. I'm relieved because I'm certain this is her effort to explain her negative reaction on Katie's special day. There *has* to be a logical reason.

June: Ken has always loved ALL of his kids very much and wanted to make sure that they each felt confident in themselves. He spent A LOT of time with each of them. A LOT more than most fathers. Granted there is a negative side to him that caused a lot of arguments that probably shouldn't have happened but he claims all people argue. He said your parents did it also. I'm sorry Katie only remembers the negative about us. Deep down he really wants the best for everybody and is a decent guy.

Bounding up from my chair, I pace the room, kicking balls and other exercise tools out of the way, fuming as I do so. Does she actually believe what she just wrote? Comparing 'people arguing' to fights with Ken is like saying a light breeze has the same effect as a tornado. If June buys into this analogy, then we've surely lost her to his poison.

Survivor's guilt surfaces once again. After all, June did take my place as Ken's primary victim. I remember first meeting her when she was young, hopeful, and so enamored by him.

*****

Sitting in my car with my future sister-in-law, I am delirious that Ken is getting married. It came as a surprise since they haven't dated long, and Ken is only 23 years old. But June is kind and friendly and we have easily bonded as family. She must know him differently than I do because all of her actions point to how in love she is. In a few short weeks. he will be with her and hopefully less focused on me.

"I'm beginning to think your brother has a dark side," she blurts out as we idle in the mall parking lot one afternoon.

"He flips out on me for no reason," June sighs deeply.

I hold my breath.

"Does he have a temper?" A direct question from her. Now I have to answer.

"He does," I state simply, already feeling the apprehension that comes from saying anything bad about Ken, knowing that somehow it will boomerang back to hurt me.

"How bad is it?" she continues to probe.

I desperately search my mind to find a way to understate his darkness and wiggle out of this conversation. Instead, an uncontained hysteria washes over me like a tidal wave.

"Get out while you can!" explodes from my mouth, and I don't even recognize my voice. "He's an evil monster!"

Then comes THE LOOK. THE LOOK of pity, of defensiveness, of mistrust. THE LOOK that always coats people's faces when I speak the truth about Ken. It comes from my parents, from my parents' peers, from most of my friends, and from a few therapists. And now June is also giving me THE LOOK.

"I don't think he's THAT bad, Mary. Do you think you are overreacting?"

She drops the conversation.

———

"How dare you, Mary," my mother reprimands the next day. "June told me what you said about Ken. Why do you hate him so much?"

"I like June, Mom. I told her the truth."

"Do NOT sabotage the wedding, Mary. It's none of your business."

"She ASKED me, Mom."

"But your view is skewed because you don't like him. I told her just that."

———

It is a surreal moment as we sit at the rehearsal dinner. I find it strange to be placed next to Ken, but since everyone is so joyous, I let it go. The wedding is tomorrow and there is an excitement in the air that lifts even me up. Maybe this will be good for Ken. Maybe I HAVE been too hard on him.

His eyes burn into the side of my head and command me to face him. Fear smothers me as I turn to see a look in his eyes that is not quite human. A combination of puppy dog and coldness; sappy, yet threatening. A spasm emits from my core.

Ken leans toward me and whispers without even a blink, "I'm getting married, Mary. But you will always be the only woman for me."

Spitting up my water while running to the bathroom, I slam the stall door and gasp for air. I told June to get out. I did my part, and she chose to stay. She now MUST become his new target, or I will not be able to go on. I will pray for that.

*****

I try to physically shake my body, rubbing muscles until they are on fire to rid them of the guilt. June didn't get away like I did. And now she is brainwashed against Katie. Am I somehow to blame for that? Has Katie lost her mom for good because of me?

———

#%@/>#%\@ calling...

It's a few days after Katie's birthday. I wait for the text.

Ken: Facebook goes all over the world Mary, is your stupid brain aware of that? June has pictures of you with Katie at a birthday party, a party you were insisting never happened and you went on and on pretending this while knowing we had a party planned for Katie first. Instead of trying to get Katie reconciled with her own parents like decent people do you tried and are still trying to become Katie's surrogate mother. Both civil and criminal lawyers say you have no chance. You can only screw with people so much before they will defend themselves Mary. If you don't admit what you are doing then we will proceed to the next stage. This is for real. It is not a TV show.

CHAPTER 15

KATIE:

I wake to a bright light shining in my face, and it takes a couple moments before I realize that I forgot to close the curtains the night before. I dozed off late last night on the couch with Herbie, Grandpa's cat, on my lap. It wasn't until 3:00 in the morning that I actually made my way up to bed.

I groan at the morning light, trying my very best to reach up to close the drapes without moving the position of my body. My arm extends upward at an awkward angle. and I try to see what I am doing with one eye squinted shut, unable to open them completely yet. I finally reach the drapes and pull them closed, my body relaxing into the fluffy depths of the pillows once more. I reach for my phone on the side of my bed to check the time, and as I grasp it, it slips. I attempt to catch it again, this time opening both of my eyes, but just miss it as it falls down between the bed and the wall, a space far too small for my hand. I close my eyes in frustration, realizing that my extra hour of sleep just isn't happening today.

When I finally check the time, I see that I don't have to be at the Loft for another 90 minutes. This is a change from my usual morning routine consisting of rolling out of bed right before I am supposed to leave.

Dad has been harassing me and everyone else non-stop. He's been texting, calling, and making weekly visits since he found out that I was actually living with Grandpa and Stuart. It has been getting worse since my birthday last week. Mary told me she got a bunch of 'torture texts' from him about the last-minute party she arranged for me. One of the guests tagged me in a photo on Facebook. Mom saw it and of course showed it to Dad. I don't see why this was such a big deal. I haven't spent the last four or five birthdays with them since I was away at school.

Stuart tells me that every weekend when they come here, Dad beelines to this very bedroom and searches it, looking for signs of me or any of my possessions—what little possessions I own, that is. Fortunately, I have remained one step ahead. Grandpa has been miraculously laying down the law with Dad, demanding advanced warning to show up here, even though I now expect it to be every weekend. When he comes, I continue the same routine as I did when I first got here: pack up my backpack and put everything in the room in its designated place. No book unturned, no crinkle in the duvet.

Mary gifted me a few articles of clothing from Grandma. Most of her stuff didn't fit right, as she was quite a bit heavier than me in her later years, but I was particularly excited about an extra-large Green Bay Packers sweatshirt. It still had the new feel and smell to it, probably not even worn because it definitely didn't fit her style of dress blouses and slacks. But I love it and wear it and, since it belonged to Grandma, it is special.

I was rushed packing up last time so instead of transferring everything into my car, I decided to put some stuff in drawers. I remember folding the Packers sweatshirt ever so neatly, the way Sylvia would have—no corner sticking out, no unnecessary creases. I placed it in the bottom drawer, making it look like it had been there a long time, perhaps due to lack of storage in Grandma's room. I figured it would be safe since it looked like it had been there for quite a while.

The drawer was empty when I got home last night. I searched the entire room to see if it had been moved elsewhere. I even asked Grandpa if he had seen it. When I discovered that it was nowhere to be found, it became clear exactly what happened. Dad took it.

It may have been a small item that I only owned for a short amount of time, but I feel invaded, as though my personal privacy has been ripped from beneath me. It's one thing to come here every single weekend when I clearly am trying to get distance from him, but to rummage through the drawers I'm using takes it to another level. He has no right to any of it, any of me. I hate that he considers me, his fully grown and educated daughter, a possession. My skin itches and I want to crawl right out of it at the thought.

The pressure is building the longer I stay here. Dad claims others are keeping me from him and he has 'no clue why', as if I have no mind of my own. He knows the harm he has inflicted, both the day after Grandma's funeral and our whole lives. But to make it clear one more time, I have been working on a letter to him. Mary thinks it is a good idea. I worry that she is getting too much pressure for defending me, and if this letter can alleviate some of it, then so much the better.

Sitting at my desk staring at the jumbled notes I have started, I ask myself what I actually want from him. If I come on too strong and blame him, then he will find fault in that. I have to show him that this is not out of hate. I begin writing feverishly and don't stop until I sign 'Sincerely, Katie' at the end.

Dear Dad,

I wanted to write this letter to you to give you a deeper understanding of what has been going on this past month or so. As you have noticed, I am no longer living with you and Mom, and I do not respond to your texts and calls. I want to help you understand why that is, and why I left that awful night after Grandma's funeral. In this letter, you will find what I need from you.

I will try my best to be as straightforward as possible.

I will start with the night I left. There were a couple of different factors that drove me out of the house then. First off, you were caught in the act of doing something very wrong and illegal. But not only that, you proceeded to deny it to us when we had video and audio recordings of it. We as a family were tired of those sort of things happening, so that's why we were so insistent at first that you admit you have a problem. However, what propelled me out of the house was not your actions alone, but Mom's and Sandra's. They thought the best thing to do was to forgive you almost instantly. While I agree that forgiveness is in fact a key part of a happy life, I don't believe that was the issue at hand. To forgive in that moment would have actually been more like 'sweeping the problem under the rug', not actually cleaning it up. I realized that I wasn't okay with doing that anymore. The mess that had collected from years and years of brushing it out of sight had begun to seep out from underneath 'the rug' until it was unbearable. You were attempting to buy drugs that were not prescribed to you. When we caught you, you screamed and became verbally abusive to all of us, demanding money that you had done nothing to earn.

Not only were you verbally abusive to Mom and Sandra, you were especially cruel to me. You told me that I am a despicable human being. You pointed your finger directly at me and said "You! You are no longer my daughter!" And then later that night, after it had calmed down a bit, I cried in the other room wishing for you to get help. And while I was in there, you came in and told me, "Yeah, you better cry." As if it gave you no better pleasure than to see me in pain.

What is so crazy about that night is that I was actually the quietest of the three of us. I told you that your actions were wrong, yes. But I was not nearly as vocal as the others. Sandra even screamed in your face a few times, begging for you to see how hurt we all were and still are. And yet, it was me who was told I am despicable.

No big deal, right? I should be used to that sort of thing by now. That is how you have treated me my entire life. Why should it bother me? Well the thing is, despite the numerous occasions this has happened, it doesn't make it okay. In fact, it makes it much worse.

The world I believe in is one where people treat others with respect. The individuals in this world say affirmations to build the ones they love up, not deliver insults to tear them down. The world I believe in has those who do things for others without expecting anything in return. This world is filled with love, not hate.

I used to think I hated you, that I genuinely didn't love a single bone in your body. This escalated tremendously in the past few years. How can I love a person who most of the time wants to crush me? How can I love someone who wants to make me cry? How can I love someone who always takes and rarely gives? How can I love someone who doesn't love himself? I have thought about these questions over and over, for a long time truly believing I did not love my own father.

But then I started talking to people—about me, about you, about the rest of the family. They empathized with me and shared stories of their own. The more I talked I began to realize something. It's not that I don't love you. It's that I hate the actions you choose to do.

I HATE how you choose to treat others because of your pain. I HATE that you take out your anger and sadness on everyone around you. I

HATE that you are always taking but rarely giving anything back. I HATE that my entire life knowing you has been controlled by an addiction of some sort of yours. And finally, I HATE who I become around you. It's always the worst side of me and it scares me.

Despite all this that I desperately hate, I do not hate YOU. When you treat others poorly, I know that is not my real dad. Truth be told, I love you, Dad, and I want nothing more than for you to get better.

I am fully aware that this letter seems harsh at some points and that you are probably thinking of all the things I have done wrong too. Because believe me, I am aware that I am flawed. However, the issue in this case is not perfection, but rather addiction and other mental illnesses. I have learned my limits and I need you to make serious changes for me to be in your life again.

To be completely blunt, what I am looking for is for you to go to inpatient rehab and get clean, Dad. 100%. I want my father off all the addictive painkillers, even legitimate prescriptions. I have been doing research on inpatient care facilities and I know they will

treat your pain. Just not in the way you are
used to.

I know you are in a lot of physical discomfort
since your hands accident, and I'm sorry for
this. I also know that this process of detox, while
you are in that kind of pain, will possibly be
one of the hardest things you will ever do. But
I hope you know that if you go through with it,
you would not only have my complete support,
but the entire family's as well. We all want you
to feel better; and while there is no guarantee
that this will do that, I would not be able to live
with myself if I just gave up without trying
everything in my power to stop this destructive
path you are on.

So now that you know what I want, it is up to
you to decide what is next. I want a dad that
tells me things like 'hope is everything', and
'never settle for less than you deserve' and
actually believes it, demonstrates it, lives it. I
want you to walk me down the aisle someday
completely detoxed and clean. I believe that is
my true dad, not the mean person you show
to the world.

I hope you see this letter as not malicious, but
rather as one last cry for you to get help. I

don't want to live life fatherless, and I really hope that will not be the case.

I love you, Dad. Please take care of yourself.

Sincerely, Katie

As I shake out the cramp in my hand, I look it over a few times. The message finally seems right. I will see what Mary thinks after class.

MARY:

"Wow." I take a deep breath to absorb what I just read. "That's a wonderful, moving, loving, yet firm letter, Katie." We are sitting in our usual spot on the stage at the Loft, after one of the morning classes, when Katie shares the final version of what she wants to send to her dad.

"Do you think there is any wiggle room for him?" Katie knows it has to be twist-proof.

"I can't see it if there is." I peruse the pages again as I answer. "Besides, it's so touching I cannot believe your father wouldn't want to try to get better for you."

"Well, it's never worked before, even when I was about eight." Katie's eyes well up.

*****

KATIE:

I am crushed. A couple days ago when we went to my brother's basketball tournament, I lost my new teddy bear. He was orange but tinted white, depending on which direction you looked at him. He looked like a roasting marshmallow atop an open flame, so naturally I named him 'Marshmallow on Fire', or 'M.F.' for short. I had just gotten him for my birthday, and he immediately became one of the gang, which also includes my stuffed elephant 'Elephy' and his bunny friend 'Bully'. They are some of my best friends.

But now, M.F. is lost and my heart is broken. What if he is hurt? Is he scared to be out on his own? Is he trying to find his way back home? These are all questions I keep asking Mom, so we are now on our way to the store to pick up another toy to replace him. I think Mom is trying to cheer me up, but all I feel is sadness that my friend is out there without me.

However, as we arrive at the toy store and enter the stuffed animal aisle, I see a familiar friend staring at me. M.F. is here! And he is surrounded by tons of other marshmallow friends of all colors and sizes. Words can't describe the relief I feel that he has been okay this whole time, and from the looks of it, he even grew a little bit. Wow! Mom asks if I would like one of the purple or green marshmallow bears, but I refuse instantly. I needed my M.F. back, not some other strangely colored bear.

We take M.F. 2.0 to the register and start our trek back home. I am still in awe that we were able to get him back, so I quietly hug him and stare at him happily in the back seat. This is such an amazing feeling! I wish for everyone to feel as good as M.F. and I do at this moment. I wish it for Mom, my brother, and my sister. I realize that I mostly wish it for Dad.

Dad doesn't get happy all that often, and it makes me very sad. I think it is the alcohol that makes him angry…at least that is what Mom always tells me. I don't know why the return of M.F. gets me thinking about this, but now I can't seem to get it off my mind. I start to cry. When we get home, Mom notices my tears.

"What's wrong, sweetie? I thought you liked your bear," she says while trying to comfort me with hug.

"I want … Daddy … to stop … drinking," I respond in between sobs. I don't think I have ever wanted anything more.

"Oh honey," she says soothingly, but with a lost look on her face. She pulls me tighter into her arms. "I want that, too, so very bad."

"I don't want him to get hurt, Mommy." I'm crying out for the fear and sadness I feel for Dad.

"How about we tell Daddy this together?" she asks me gently, and I agree almost immediately.

"Here, just take a seat on the bed, and I will go get him." I look at her and nod with tears pooling in my eyes, never letting M.F. out of my arms. The next thing I know, Mom enters the room again, followed by Dad.

"Ken, your daughter is very upset and would like to tell you something," Mom starts the conversation.

Dad, seeing my tears, comes over and sits next to me on the bed. He looks confused.

"What would you like to tell me?" Even though he seems very loving now, I can't help but feel a little nervous.

"I don't want you to drink alcohol, Daddy. I don't want you to die from it," I whisper as another sniffle comes out.

"Well, I am definitely not going to die, Katie. You know that, right?" Dad sounds so sure.

"I...guess... so." I'm barely able to speak now. "I am just so scared that the alcohol will kill you."

"Well, I want you to know that your dad is a pretty tough guy. And he is not going anywhere." He puts an arm around me.

"But does it really bother you that much that I drink?" he asks, and I nod for a long time. It bothers me so very much.

"Well, it's not going to be easy, but I will try to quit. I promise." Dad looks me straight in the eyes as he says this.

"Okay," I say as the sobs lessen and I feel hope move through me again.

This is the best day ever! First, M.F. is back home and now Dad is going to quit drinking for me. I hug M.F. tighter than ever now that I'm alone again. I always knew he was a special friend, but today after his reappearance in our household, he has really brought some magic to this family. He is my positive omen, my good luck charm.

*****

MARY:

"Wow," I say again. "You've wanted to get him help for a very long time. Another way that we are alike. I started pleading with my mom around the same age to do something."

*****

"IT's back."

Oh no, not again. I don't like it when Ken gets like this. Sometimes he can be such a fun older brother. He's so smart and handsome, and I admire him so much. I am only eight, but he is a full ten years old, so he is waaaay wiser than me. But when IT comes back, everything gets dark.

"What's back, Kenny?" my mom asks as she does every other time he says these words.

"IT. The monster inside of me." He sounds scary.

"Oh Kenny, don't be so dramatic." Her regular response.

I am worried. I don't like IT being back. I plop myself outside his locked bedroom door and wait for the darkness to pass. I hear the shades close and see the light go out underneath the door. He is moaning words now. "Make it go away, make it go away…"

"Kenny, can you come out and play?" I yell through the locked door. No answer. "Kenny please?" Silence.

Fear takes over. I can usually get through to him. I scurry down the stairs to the kitchen where my mom is making dinner.

"Please help Kenny, Mommy…something's wrong with him."

"What do you mean?" she asks without taking her eyes off what she is doing.

"He's in his room talking to himself, and he keeps telling it to go away."

"He's probably telling YOU to go away, Mary. You know he doesn't like to be bothered when he's in his room."

"No, this is worse, Mommy. Something's wrong. He's in his room all the time now. Can you please go see him and help him? Please please please?"

"You and your brother are two completely different people. Just because you like to be out of your room and with people doesn't mean there is something wrong with him. Leave him alone, Mary."

*****

"That's exactly what my mom always says, too," Katie reveals. "Just leave him alone." Katie pauses but I can tell she wants to say more. It's as if a lightbulb goes on in her head as she asks, "Wait... how long has my dad been sick?"

I answer as honestly as I can, knowing there will be no denial or accusations of exaggeration with Katie. "I think he was born mentally ill. Grandma would never admit that, but I've heard from some of her siblings and a couple of her long-time friends that your dad didn't move as a baby much. He seldom made noises and there was little to no eye contact. Grandma could set him on the couch at the age of one, and he would sit for hours just staring. She thought she had 'the best child in the world', never occurring to her that this is not normal baby behavior. Then when I came along he just got lost in the shuffle. Grandma had her hands full with my digestive problems; plus, once I got older, I was the complete opposite of

Ken—very energetic, talkative, even hyperactive, although not officially diagnosed. If he wasn't *born* mentally ill, then my arrival certainly triggered multiple problems. Grandma always said the latter."

Katie interrupts me. "Grandma blamed your birth for his illness?"

"She did," I say succinctly. It still hurts to admit that, though.

"That's ridiculous." I can see the fire in Katie's eyes that surfaces every time another item of family lunacy gets shared in our conversations.

"What is especially crazy is that even if it were true that I caused his mental problems, to constantly tell me just that really did a number on my psyche," I continue. "Grandma used it as a way to get me to be nicer to him. For most of my life I felt I needed to make it up to him, even though I couldn't help that I was born, or how I was as a baby."

"That's so messed up, Mary," Katie says with genuine empathy.

I'm encouraged to finish out the picture for Katie. "When your dad was a teenager, everything got worse. He no longer was shy and silent, but rather had drastic mood swings and violent outbursts. And such anger. The social workers at high school referred my parents to a highly regarded psychiatrist at Northwestern Hospital. They actually took him there. After just a couple of visits, this doctor said that Ken was severely ill on multiple mental levels and needed to be hospitalized immediately for a full workup."

"So… a mental institution?" Katie's eyes open wide with shock.

"Yes." I am succinct again to let this information sink in.

"So what happened?" Katie clearly wants to know everything.

"Grandma and Grandpa got scared. They called this guy a *quack*. They took your dad home and went into incredulous denial about their son for decades. Just about a year before Grandma died, she actually admitted—and only once—that *'in hindsight that doctor was right'*. I nearly fell off my chair when she said that. But we never spoke of it again."

"Wow." Katie is now the succinct one.

We go silent after this bonding moment—one of many that keep occurring as we get to know each other. We are so alike I can hardly believe what I'm hearing at times. Someone on the inside who sees it my way. Finally.

Maybe now we will be heard, and Ken will get the help he needs.

CHAPTER 16

MARY:

"This is awful," Katie sighs to the counselor we are now seeing to deal with the stress. "The family is completely divided into two teams because of me. It seems like it's me and Mary against everyone else, though a few go back and forth." She looks over at me for confirmation.

"I agree." The heaviness of this overwhelms me. "June is in his web. The other two siblings are torn but staying out of it. Stuart feels bad for Ken. My dad is being sucked back onto Ken's team with Ken's constant obsessive phone calls. *'Are you ever going to talk to your father again?'* he keeps asking Katie in his critical and judgmental tone. Or *'Can't you at least say hello?'*"

"I thought Grandpa understood, but instead I get guilt comments like that," Katie says mournfully. "I tried to show by the letter that I want to help him."

"We are stuck," I say as I resign myself to the pathetic fact that no one else really wants to help Ken in the way he needs. Even the letter didn't have much impact.

We are silent for quite some time, each lost in our heads. Then Katie blurts out, "How about we try an intervention?"

My stomach curdles from the term. Sandra lived with my parents for a while during college. She came to me with similar distressing thoughts about her dad. She wanted to do something at the time as well. I realize with discouragement how long this topic has existed. Why can't Ken ever get help? If he won't do so himself, why don't the rest of us step up?

"We tried that when Sandra was living here," I divulge. "I organized it, but she was the catalyst. She wanted to help him, but your mom backed out at the last minute. Grandma told her '*fixing Ken was Mary's agenda. She's been out to get him for a long time*.'"

"But Grandma isn't here, and my mom wouldn't have to know until it actually is happening." Katie's hope emanates from her heart.

I hate this.

I don't want to do this again.

I need to stay out of it.

But... I *do* have Katie to back me this time. Maybe she has more 'pull' with the others.

"Okay... we can try again," I concede reluctantly. We have to keep attempting to help him.

———

Katie forwards the letter to her siblings and asks them to join us for what we are calling a 'family meeting' as opposed to an intervention. Sandra and Josh agree cautiously, thinking it won't work. "But what if it actually does?" Katie presses convincingly. My dad, surprisingly, is all for it, but Stuart is not. Terry is willing to come to protect me but thinks it's a waste of time.

Katie and I spend hours coaching the players in the intervention. We need to be united. One weak link in the chain and it will fail. We have to be clear that we want him in rehab and completely off drugs. We also spend a considerable amount of time researching facilities in his area that can help him. We are exhausted from this topic, yet there is an energy driving us that maybe… possibly… hopefully…this will finally make him better. It's a long shot, but we have to keep trying.

———

My head pounds and my legs shake as I head up the porch stairs to my dad's house on the day of the intervention. Stuart is gone, Sandra is on speaker phone from L.A., and the rest of us await Ken and June's arrival. My dad invited them down on the pretense to talk with Katie, not telling them about the rest of us. My instincts are screaming at me to run away. Instead, I sit in the circle with the rest of them to wait. Anticipation tightens my rib cage.

Out the front window I see Ken's plodding gait as he struggles with the stairs. For years now he walks as if he is twice as heavy and half as tall. He grunts with each step and sighs like he cannot go on. As the door opens, I hold my breath. He takes in the group and explodes.

"NO WAY, NO WAY, NO WAY! I KNOW WHAT THIS IS—I'M NOT AN IDIOT! You really believe I'm going to stay for this? Come on, June, let's go."

"Hold on, Ken." June grabs his arm in an attempt to calm him, but he's pacing like a caged animal. He throws her off. "DON'T TOUCH ME, DAMMIT!"

He barges out the front door and heads toward the car, but then turns and charges back into the house. "YOU ARE AWFUL, HORRIBLE PEOPLE FOR DOING THIS TO ME!"

"Calm down, Ken." My dad attempts to sound stern.

"Just hear us out, Dad." Josh's tone is flat and robotic, like he's already tired of this.

"Dad… Can I say something?" We all look toward the voice, but no one is seated there. We look at each other, then back to the chair. Katie's phone is on the seat… that's where she had set Sandra.

"Can anybody hear me?" the chair speaks again. For some reason we all start laughing. Even Ken semi-smiles.

For a moment the mood lightens. Ken plops with a thud onto the couch. "Hi Sandra," he says sweetly, as he has always had a soft spot for her. But that is short-lived, and he erupts again. "YOU!" He points aggressively at Terry as he struggles to get up. "YOU ARE NOT ALLOWED TO BE HERE. YOU ARE NOT PART OF THE FAMILY!" He falls back into the couch while yelling. Squirming in his seat, he kicks the coffee table as he finally heaves his bloated body up and stomps out of the room.

The rest of us sit still, defeated. My heart is racing, and I can hardly catch a good breath.

The refrigerator door opens and the familiar crack of the Pepsi can tells us that Ken is down in the family room. We hear the rattle of pill bottles, knowing without seeing that he is popping a random mixture of several at a time, as always. Time stands still as we wait for his next move. A good five minutes passes without hearing a sound from him. Then, as if nothing bothered him at all, he strolls back in with the group, flops down in his spot, and with an already present slur he says, "So what do you want to talk about?"

We spend about an hour individually telling him we love him and highlighting his good qualities. It is awkward and forced, but I can see Katie is hopeful. She is the last to speak, opening the letter and reading one part:

"To be completely blunt, what I am looking for is for you to go to inpatient rehab and get clean, Dad. 100%. I want my father off all the addictive painkillers, even legitimate prescriptions. I have

BEEN DOING RESEARCH ON INPATIENT CARE
FACILITIES AND I KNOW THEY WILL TREAT
YOUR PAIN. JUST NOT IN THE WAY YOU ARE
USED TO."

"There is NOOOO WAY!" Ken cuts Katie off. "You have no fucking clue the amount of pain I am in. Do you really hate me that much that you want me to suffer?"

"I told you in the letter that I don't hate you, Dad," Katie stays remarkably composed and looks him straight in the eyes. "I'm doing this out of love."

"Bullshit!" He spits as he yells this.

"I want you clean, Dad." Katie remains strong.

This is the point where his other kids are supposed to jump in and agree. Neither child utters a word. I am about to encourage them to do so, but June speaks before I can.

"Now, Katie, maybe it doesn't have to be so extreme. He needs *some* pills."

"I agree," admits my dad.

No, no, no… we cannot give him wiggle room, I say to them in my head. Trying to redirect the conversation, I insert "They would figure that out in rehab."

"Shut up, Mary." Ken's anger toward me still hurts at my core.

"How about an outpatient program?" The chair speaks again.

No, Sandra, I say again in my head.

"Did you look into those, Katie?" Josh pipes in.

They are softening.

This is bad.

This is not going to work.

"YOU SEE? I'm not the problem here, Katie! You let Mary brainwash you, and now you are both out to get me. And by the way, you have a temper, too. You hit me. You broke my back."

Holy shit, he's turning himself into the victim again.

"Whaaaat?" My dad looks to Katie.

"I slapped you Dad, yes," she admits, calm on the exterior but I can tell that accusation hurt. "But you have done way worse to us for as long as I can remember. And I'm certain that slap could not break your back."

"Well, there is no reason for any hitting at all," June states.

This from a woman who has accepted Katie standing voluntarily between her and her husband trying to keep him from doing just that.

"Dad, can we get back to the point of this meeting?" Katie sounds firm.

"NO, WE CANNOT! I WILL NOT SPEAK TO YOU AS LONG AS YOU ARE UNDER THE INFLUENCE OF THAT!" Ken jabs both forefingers toward me, but it's his eyes that throw daggers and scare me into silence.

I tune out… the level of anger he exudes is colossal. My brain starts to hum a tune, and I completely exit the room in my mind.

And then we are done. Everyone is getting up. Only Katie and her parents remain. Ken is laughing and trying to look cute. He looks pleadingly at Katie and says, "Can I have a hug?"

My mind goes blank . . . I don't remember anything between my dad's house and the Loft. I 'wake up' halfway through the yoga class I am now teaching. My head spins as I try to maintain control of my physical body. I go into auto-pilot to finish the class. When the last student leaves, I collapse onto the floor and try to breathe, passing out from fatigue.

Chapter 17

KATIE:

I am emotionally drained. We put a lot of work into that intervention and nothing is going to change. Dad will not be going to an inpatient facility. He will not be seeing a therapist. He is still going to take his prescription drugs. I am beginning to wonder what the point was. All I got out of it was him making me feel worse about myself after working so hard to rally everyone together. *You have a temper, too, Katie.* My body aches as irritation grows every time I think about him telling me that. I didn't want to prove him right, so I swallowed it down the way I would sip hot soup. And it burned my insides as it travelled to the pit of my stomach. I chose not to defend myself because I know it was him trying to get to me. It may have worked, but he didn't need to know that. I didn't want to act like him.

I wish my family would have stuck together like we said we would, but as soon as he started to fight back in the way that he does, everyone softened. They fell back into the habit of letting down their guard to 'keep the peace' for the night. I guess habits are harder to break than I thought. And now the only thing agreed upon was for Dad to start healthier habits and to supposedly have check-ins *every so often*. I roll my eyes at the lack of structure. We didn't even set up the first follow-up meeting. It seems like everyone just wanted to get out of there.

My parents seem to think that I will talk to them again, but when I tried to 'suck it up' and do so after the intervention, it didn't feel right. It still doesn't. Dad may have left in good spirits because he got off far easier than he should have, but nothing was resolved. I need more time to sort out how I feel about this, but I want to try to be communicative with them about my intent. I want to be mature and up front with handling this.

I pull out my phone and send Mom and Dad a group text:

Katie: I apologize for leaving so abruptly yesterday. I am just not ready to have a proper relationship with either of you yet. I am glad we all talked and that steps are being taken for a better lifestyle. I hope it will continue. However, I am still feeling very hurt, and I need time away. I am asking that you both respect that and give me the space I ask for. This is not out of hate, I am just not ready for anything else.

I don't know how they will respond. I want to be able to have a relationship with them, but at the same time, the thought brings me crippling anxiety. Only a few minutes pass and my phone buzzes. I don't find myself surprised to see Dad's name show up, not Mom's.

Ken: We are feeling very hurt too. Neither one of us is sure if you realize that.

I am disappointed by his words even though I expected the sentiment. This response shows exactly the type of person he is. He can never own up to the things he has done wrong. I only requested space from him, which I don't think is too much to ask. I text him back:

Katie: Understood. I still need space for my own needs. Respect that please.

Ken: And respect that we raised you to adulthood. Respect means you are not rude to your parents after everyone else leaves. If you can't handle being polite for two or three lousy minutes then maybe we should be asking if Katie wants her parents ever in her life again. In fact, it is a question that is already being asked.

I am doing this to protect myself. I don't want to only be good and kind when I am not around him. He brings out the worst in me, but I want to be good all the time. I can't change him, but I can't honestly accept him either. Maybe someday I can forgive him for his wrongdoings, but today is not that day. As I ruminate, my phone buzzes once more.

Ken: We don't want the Katie in our lives that shows us no respect at all as you have done these past two months. It hurts too much. You have been miserable to us Katie and we have had it.

I don't even bother responding. To a normal person, giving space would be acceptable. If someone feels remorse about hurting another person, space would be a no-brainer. The only no-brainer here, though, is that my father doesn't have remorse, no matter how much I wish he did.

———

The week passes slowly. I have completely stopped responding to texts from Dad as they get more outlandish each time. One of them comes through just as I am pulling into Grandpa's driveway after work tonight. I read it in my car with the engine still running.

Ken: As I sit here texting your mom is in the hospital recovering from a colonoscopy. Just a little while ago the heart monitor went off and it scared me but was a false alarm. Might be a nice gesture if you called her today showing concern for her and not for yourself. Just a suggestion.

I roll my eyes as I try to piece together his logic and realize once again that there is none. Mom supposedly got a colonoscopy that none of us knew about, and from that her heart monitor goes off… for what? Being able to poop properly again? The only shit coming from this new story is bullshit. Now that I have had some distance from him and have been sticking to it, I don't believe a word he says.

I shut off my phone, sick of all the negativity coming from it, and climb out of my Honda. When I get inside, Stuart is in the living room watching TV. We greet each other briefly before I sit down and join him.

"I hear my dad is coming this weekend for Easter," I say to him. He immediately turns off the TV and takes a deep breath. We have only talked a few times since I began staying here, but in the last couple months alone it is probably more than the total I have spoken to him my entire life.

"He is. Are you going to be leaving again?" Stuart asks more out of obligation, already knowing the answer.

"That's kind of my life, always on the run in some form." My face grins, but I don't feel joy.

Stuart nods his head in agreement. "That's quite unfortunate. If it counts for anything, I would prefer you to be here over him. You are doing the right thing by staying away from him."

"Thanks, Stuart." If that was the case, why couldn't he have shown up at the intervention a few days ago? I don't ask him though because he has already told us that he didn't see the point. He was probably right, given how it turned out.

"Even if you are always leaving when he comes around, you are truly a wonderful niece." Stuart sounds sincere.

My eyes dart over to him, surprised at his words. I wasn't expecting that. "Thank you. That is very nice of you to say."

"You have probably become my favorite kid of his just with these conversations about him and everything," Stuart continues.

"Well, that certainly wasn't the goal, but the sentiment is surely appreciated," I say with a laugh.

We sit in silence and I can't help but reflect. Never in my life did I think that Stuart and I would have a moment like this. He was always my weird uncle, nothing more. But now he is actually becoming a sort of friend.

Somehow the topic changes to Thanksgiving last year, and how it was nice to have one more holiday with Grandma still alive.

"You know, the best part about that day was the picture that we all took together. Have I ever showed you it?" I say with a smirk on my face.

"No, you have not." Stuart is always thoroughly blunt.

"Well, first of all, you all were so mad at me for taking it because the food was getting cold. It definitely shows. But you were probably the funniest part of it because your frown was the biggest." I can feel laughter seep out as I scroll through the pictures on my phone, finally finding it. I zoom in on Stuart's face. For some reason the camera distorted it so that it looked bigger than usual and in the shape of a long oval. On top of that, his face contains a massive frown as if there was nothing he'd rather do less than take a picture with the whole family.

As soon I show it to him, he bursts out into a loud cackle. We sit there laughing like that for at least five minutes, the comic relief a nice respite from the tense topic of Dad.

I go up to my room, amazed at the family I didn't know I had. Even in this hard time, we still find a way to laugh.

There remains a small bit of hope for us all.

CHAPTER 18

MARY:

The Fitness Loft is always upbeat and fun, but Saturdays are the most festive. The mix of peeps is more varied than during the week, and that dynamic creates even more laughter and vibrant socialization than usual. Today, being the day before Easter, is especially celebratory since many visiting family members are joining the workouts as guests.

As I watch the Weights class being taught by one of my trainers, I take in the picture in front of me. I'm so beholden to this place, this wonderful group of friends, my beautiful studio, my life's work playing out before my eyes. Once again, the contrast of this compared to the lunacy of the Albrechts strikes me hard. Especially now that the same lunacy is back in my life, it is evident how far I have come. I cannot let myself slip back into that horrible place where I was trapped by the dysfunctional mania. But it seems like all I think about now as I try to help Katie get strong.

It's been a few weeks since the intervention, but surprisingly Ken has gone dormant toward me. Katie, however, is getting all the venom. She asked him for space after it failed so miserably but that's like telling a rabid dog not to bite. He's ramped up his desperation for control, and I can see his emotional abuse is taking its toll on Katie.

Easter will not be acknowledged this year since we are completely torn up as a unit. Ken and June will be down, of course, being that Libertyville is another addiction Ken has, especially since Katie arrived. She will have to pack up and leave the house again—a reflection of the ridiculous nature of us. I envision my mom looking down from Heaven with sadness that we are this way, especially given that Easter was her most revered holiday. A pang of guilt hits me that, somehow, I caused this shattered mess, and I try to force my thoughts away from that familiar role by reminding myself that Katie is in this with me. Thank God for that. She validates the absurdity.

I snap out of the darkness when both my kitties demand my attention. They came to me in the form of rescues at the best possible time—right before my mom got sick. I couldn't save my mom, but I could save them. They consistently pull me into the present moment and soothe my soul. Noticing the time, I jump out of the chair to get ready for the next class since I am the one teaching it. "Come on, Bern and Bell, breakfast," I call in my high-talk voice. I head toward the back room with them galloping behind to catch up.

Once I begin the Yoga warm-up I instantly feel better, lighter, happier. I'm glad I don't have to deal with family stress this weekend. I plan to lick my wounds from the past few months. Maybe I will actually have time to myself. I've forgotten what that looks like.

After the last peep has left, I flop down on the stage and embrace the silence. Finally a chance to breathe. I pick up my phone to turn it back on so I can order some food and read. I can't wait to nap after lunch. I'm going to make this a great day.

When the screen lights up, my peace turns to panic when Terry's text appears.

Terry: Your dad had a stroke. I'm with him in the ER. Get here when you can.

Moments like this cause everything to stop, including my breathing. It takes a bit for this to register, but when it does, my head begins to swirl. The stress, oh my God, we did this to him. Ken did it to him. The poor man just lost his wife; he shouldn't have such a broken family. Shit— Ken is going to freak—he will use this to his advantage somehow, I am sure. I have to warn Katie. And I guess I also need to tell Ken so he doesn't come here tomorrow for Easter. But in reality, I know an iron curtain won't keep him away.

My fingers shake as I text Katie. She is at work at a local chiropractic office and won't be able to talk or even see the text until later. But I have to let her know and then get over to the hospital. So much for time to myself.

KATIE:

It's slow at the chiropractic office on this day before Easter Sunday. I'm grateful we are closing early because I've been working like a maniac for over a month now. Hopefully I can rest tonight; tomorrow will be another day that brings my parents down. Since I have asked for space, I have gotten nothing but insulting and manipulative texts from *both* of them. As usual, I will have to leave the house for the day. As I proceed to the punch clock, I turn my phone back on. There is a text from Mary:

Mary: Grandpa had a stroke. I am currently at the hospital. Call me asap.

A chill ripples through me as I immediately press the call button.

"Hey, sweetie," Mary answers after a few rings.

"Hey, how is he doing?" I'm covered in goosebumps.

"He is doing okay for now. They think they caught it early enough but only time will tell if he will recover completely," Mary reports wearily.

I'm at a loss for words. What are we going to do if something happens to Grandpa, too? "Does my dad know yet?"

"Yes, but Grandpa asked him not to come down today and to call before he does tomorrow. It's possible he won't come at all." She sounds hopeful that he will respect this. I don't want to bring her down by telling her that, with him, hope is a waste of time.

I race toward the hospital, just a few miles away. Sweat dampens my palms, and it seems like it takes a lifetime to get there even though I am running through the parking lot within ten minutes.

The hairs on the back of my neck stand up when I see Grandpa in the hospital bed, tubes and monitors everywhere. He is in intensive care. Mary enters the room carrying a couple of coffees. We embrace for a very long time, saying nothing. Grandpa slurs out my name and tries to smile, but one side of his face does not move. My knees buckle and I fall into a chair. They say all we can do is wait. Which is what we do until the staff kicks us out.

CHAPTER 19

KATIE:

*****

It's dark in my room. I have woken suddenly, and I am unsure why. My mind is foggy with the recent sleep. I look at our digital alarm clock across the room that reads 2:02AM.

Then I hear it. A voice distinguishable anywhere in the house. It's bellowing and it's deep. I know exactly what woke me.

He was drinking last night. It wasn't that bad, though, or as bad as he can get anyway. He just annoyed us while we watched a movie, slewing out minor insults to us. We could also hear him blaring Bruce Springsteen in the basement which made it difficult to focus on the movie we watched. At least he wasn't shouting—that made it more bearable. But the prospect of finishing our film in peace diminished quickly from him pestering us every five minutes.

We were in the clear last night, but he is shouting now. When he yells, the sound pierces through my entire body. He has this way of making it seem like the whole earth is shaking. We all try very hard to not give him a reason to do it. Mom always says to not fight back because it just makes him angrier. It's our way of keeping the peace.

But I can hear Mom's voice yelling this time in the room near us. Her voice is not nearly as strong or scary, but I can tell she is trying to fight back. I look over at Sandra in her bed and can just barely see the whites of her eyes open and staring at the ceiling.

"How long have you been awake from it?" I whisper over to her.

"A few minutes," she responds.

I wait to see if he will settle down just like we always do. But he only seems to get louder.

"I'm going to go in there," I finally decide out loud as I hop from the confines of my bed.

"No, don't!" Sandra protests. "Mom always says to let him end his rants on his own."

"I know, but I need to sleep. It's a school night," I say as if I really care about my fourth grade classes. In reality, I just want the yelling to stop. I make my way to the door of our room and swiftly open it. Mom and Dad's room is directly across the hallway, only a few steps away. It's not far, but it's scary with the lights off. I don't like the dark.

I feel my nerves creeping up as I scurry to their door. I raise my closed fist but hesitate before knocking. There is still so much screaming on the other side that I start to wonder if I should just turn around and hide in my bed. I have no idea what will face me or if my nine-year-old self can handle it. After a few moments of gathering my nerves, I squeeze my eyes shut once and gulp down what I think is stomach acid as my hand slowly raps on the door.

The yelling stops as I do it. I then hear his voice call out: "GO AWAY."

But I don't listen. Instead, I twist the knob and slowly crack open the door enough for my head to peek through.

I find them on the corner of the queen-sized bed inches away from each other, but not in a good way. Their room is messy as always. Sandra and I tend to keep a messy room—or I do as she would say—but my parents are a force to be reckoned with. There are piles of clothes everywhere, garbage strewn within, and in the small patches of carpet that are actually free of stuff, there are spots of cat throw-up that have most likely been there for weeks.

"Katie," Dad shouts loudly. "Shut the door, this doesn't concern you."

"No," I say more bravely than I actually feel, as my knees practically knock against one another.

"KATIE, SHUT THE DOOR," he yells again, even louder this time.

"I don't want to," I say, not really knowing what I'll get out of this. Maybe to make him stop yelling at Mom? It's probably a hopeless attempt.

"Katie, just go back to bed." Mom comes through this time. Her voice is hoarse from all the yelling and crying. I suddenly feel conflicted. I am trying to help her after all.

"No," I say again. I don't want them to keep fighting. I will take the heat if it makes them stop.

"Katie, I am going to tell you one more time. Shut. The. Damn. Door." Dad sounds menacing now, threat oozing in every syllable. And I don't know what compels me to do what I do next, but with every ounce of courage I have, I push the door all the way open, step inside their bedroom, and only then shut the door behind me. I am brave. I AM brave. I try to remember this as my entire body shakes.

And that does it for him. He leaps off the bed with pure fury in his eyes and storms his way toward me. Fear like I have never felt before floods through me as it dawns on me that he is four times the size I am. What was I thinking would happen? I immediately turn and reach for the doorknob, throw the door open, and slide my body through it. I slam it behind me just milliseconds before he approaches.

After getting what he wanted, I hear him retreat, making his way back to the bed. I stand on the other side of the door panting as adrenaline coats my entire being. I tried, I really did. Maybe I am not so brave after all.

I walk back to the shared bedroom, no longer scared of the unknown of the dark when the scariest thing out there is in my parents' room.

*****

He's in town.

I stare blankly at the page of the Harry Potter book in my hands. No matter how many times I try to submerge myself into the *Great Hall*, in ruins as the *Battle of Hogwarts* comes to a close, I end up staying on the surface. The words fall flat and become no more than the two-dimensional objects that they actually are. My mind can't get away from the text Mary sent me about an hour ago this very morning. There was no call, no warning given. Dad and Mom just decided to show up at the hospital, even though they were told to call first. I am not sure what is going to happen next, but there are three things I know for certain: It is Easter Sunday, Grandpa is recovering from a stroke, and the person who haunts me in my nightmares, and now on a daily basis, is a mere 10 minutes away.

HerbieCat sits on my lap as I continue my game of pretending to make sense of the pages in front of me. He is curled up in a ball and is so big that he almost doesn't fit. His warmth and plushy weight comforts me in the way only a good cuddle can do. I stare down at the cat and can't help but be enamored by him. I do wonder what it would be like to be him in this moment. To have the world around him closing in like a deer cornered by a couple of lions, but to still be content when there is a lap from which to steal the warmth.

Stuart is in the recliner in the other corner of the room. We've both been left with nothing to do but wait for Dad to leave the area once and for all, also both worried that he will come to this house even if Grandpa isn't here. Stuart has been muttering to himself a few times over now. Most likely speaking to my dad in his mind. He talks to himself more when he is anxious or stressed, I have learned. Stress seems to be the name of the game around here. Mary reported that Grandpa seemed bothered that Ken didn't notify him of his intention to visit in advance. Given that he just had a stroke, the timing of this kind of stress could not be worse.

"Do you think he'll come here?" I ask Stuart, unable to contain my worry any longer, but now, with a mental grimace the thought of being stuck in an endless tale from Stuart contaminating my brain.

"You know," Stuart says as he takes a deep breath, "if there is something that I learned from Ken over the years, is that you never know what to expect. I—"

"But he has no right to be here," I interrupt him. "If Grandpa is at the hospital, and I asked him to give me space, then he should not be coming over, right?"

Stuart opens his mouth again, but before he has a chance to answer, my ringtone goes off. I look down at the phone next to me on the end table and see Mary's name pop up on the screen. I answer immediately, half thankful for the interruption from Stuart about to launch into his never-ending theories about his brother. Most of the time I don't mind listening to him, but getting him to stop is the hard part. He doesn't pick up on basic social cues very well.

"Did he leave already?" I ask, really knowing the answer. Mary would never call me when he was there, given the dicey dynamic of our family.

"Yes, and we don't know for sure, but I think he is on the way to the house." I roll my eyes upon hearing the news that I was already expecting. "He seemed a little too eager to leave just now." Mary sounds stressed, too. "Terry and I are on our way there, but can you hide the River Road papers just in case? Grandpa left them all over his desk in the office."

"Oh shit, of course." The River Road house, which is now named *Rivendell* after the Last Paradise in *The Lord of the Rings*, is the house that Mary and Terry are moving into in one month's time. Dad can't know about it because, not only will he will try to claim a piece of it as his own, he will stalk me and Mary there.

"Grandpa's also worried that he left cash out on his desk. Just try to keep him from going in that room if possible," Mary instructs quickly.

"Yeah, I'll do my best." The words tumble out as doubt fills my head. How could I possibly stop him? When he wants something, he is an immovable force. I scoop Herbie off my lap as I make my way to the window restlessly, looking out only momentarily before a familiar tan Suzuki turns the corner and pulls into the driveway. My pulse suddenly escapes my heart and travels swiftly to my ears.

"Mary, they are here. I don't have time to hide the papers. I am going to have to stop them from coming in." As my breath hitches in the middle of talking to her, I wonder if I sound as panicked as I feel.

"I will be there soon with Terry," she reassures me, answering my unspoken question.

"Okay, please hurry." I watch carefully as their car doors open, my jackhammer of a heart roaring loudly in my body. "I've got to go, they are coming up the steps. I can't believe he is doing this. I have asked him for space, and Grandpa isn't even here."

"It's going to be okay. We'll be there soon," Mary says hastily before we hang up.

The two of them have reached the top step now as Dad stops to search for something in his coat pocket. Mom stands next to him and waits with a frown on her face. I look back at Stuart who is still sitting in the chair across from the foyer. He looks fearful and distant, and he has been emotionally whisper-talking to himself non-stop. There is no way he is going help me confront his maniacal older brother. I am going to have no support in stopping him from coming in this time. No Mary. No Terry. No Grandpa.

Just me.

My breath reverberates from the deep exhale I let out as I turn to face the front entryway. My mind does a quick calculation of how long it would take for me to run out the back before they see me—to sprint around the house and dive into my car before they could stop me. But then my thoughts are redirected to Harry Potter's world and all the terrible situations he gets roped into. He certainly would never run, even in life or death situations, which surely this isn't. He wasn't a coward, and neither am I. For some reason, there is time in this moment for my mind to flash back to when I was nine years old and tried to stand up to him then. I'm determined to make it end differently this time.

I pull myself up to my tallest height despite the tremors shooting up and down my legs. I silently make a promise to myself that no matter what happens, I will not stoop to Dad's level and lose my dignity. I barely have time to plan anything else as the door creaks and they both step inside. I remain in the foyer, stopping them from going further. Dad locks his eyes on mine immediately.

"Why are you guys here?" I ask them within a split second of eye contact. The tension in the atmosphere thickens, becoming almost insurmountable. Their faces hold a dumbfounded look, while their stiffened stances show the aura of defensiveness that resides within them. I stand across from them with my arms at my side as I brace for 'battle', fists clenched, the weight of my body evenly distributed on my two feet.

I catch the look on Dad's face first. A blank stare of confusion crosses his features only momentarily, before he catches himself and morphs them into an angry frown.

"What do you mean *why are we here?*" he asks me irately. Mom is behind him, still apparently stunned and in the same spot between the foyer and the outside.

"I asked you both for space a little less than two weeks ago. I have it saved in a text, actually. You have done nothing but the opposite. And now I am asking you to please leave the house in which I am staying and respect that wish." I am surprised at how calm my voice is coming across; it's smooth and strong like aged bourbon—very unlike the apparent Jell-o of my legs as I feel quivering going through them again.

"Well, we aren't here to see you, did you ever think about that?" Dad spits maliciously, as if he thinks that solves the issue I presented him. My attention directs itself to Mom standing at a slight angle behind him. She remains silent.

"Well, since Grandpa is in the hospital, I don't see the reason for you to be here when he is not," I state back, voice still unwavering.

"We are here to see Stuart." His voice escalates in tone, sharp like a dagger, but his volume remains the same level as he gestures to Stuart on the chair behind me. I turn my head to where Stuart sits with his hands folded over his belly, fidgeting and muttering to himself.

"Stuart, did you ask them to come over?" I ask him, feeling well composed. His Asperger personality makes him very literal. I can only hope that he will stay true to his character in this moment. It is a little risky to include him in this because sometimes I don't know how he is going to respond. I am hoping for the best.

"No, I did not," he answers simply, with no elaboration.

Gratitude towards him warms me as my head cocks itself towards my parents again. One of my eyebrows raises as if to say 'See?' I can see the tension in their jaws tightening as they both glare back at me.

"What gives you the right to stop us? This is not your house." Dad's voice slices through me from across the space.

"I may not own this house, but it is where I am currently living. It is also not your house," I state as a matter of fact.

"Well, do you pay rent?" His voice is at screaming level now, and my eyes involuntarily blink at the raise in volume. I remind myself to not stoop to his level—to try to stay present and not let the person I don't want to be come out like it has in the past. Like it did when I left. Like it wants to every time I'm near him. I will not be like him. I *cannot* be like him.

"No," I respond truthfully, "but both Stuart and Grandpa can attest that I do plenty for this house and the people who inhabit it. I am asking you again to please leave."

"You still can't make us leave, only Grandpa can do that." I can't believe Dad could yell any louder, but he manages to do so now.

"Maybe not, but I will get someone who can," I say defiantly.

"Who, Mary? Mary can't do shit," he spits at me. "Although she would certainly like to. She's probably brainwashing you to say these things!"

I purse my lips at his remark about Mary. Anger roars in my chest at his relentless hate towards everyone in his life, especially her, and his mindset that I can never have a mind of my own. That everything I do is because someone else *brainwashed* me to do it. I swallow it down bitterly as I remember that except for a whispering Stuart in the corner of the room, I stand alone. Everything I say is because I choose to say it. Just *me.* He is spiraling into a game of poker, doing all the mind tricks against me in order to win. For my next move, however, I am about to drop my royal flush.

"No, not Mary, or Terry either, actually," I respond, ignoring the brainwashing comment altogether. "I am talking about the cops. I have written proof of me asking you to leave me alone on several occasions and you sending me text after text of malicious responses after that. That's harassment."

He hesitates at my response, but only momentarily. "You wouldn't call the fucking cops."

I raise my eyebrows at him again. I feel strong and certain in my next statement, looking him dead in the eye without so much as a single blink.

"Try me."

Mom shifts from behind him, her first movement since they arrived. Her face scrunches in pain as she decides to finally speak, but in a volume that matches Dad's. "I can't believe you are stopping him from seeing his brother on Easter. Look at what you are doing to this family!"

I look into her seething eyes and can feel the heat from them all the way across the foyer. I used to think I needed her approval to do things in regards to him or the family, that she was a positive light amidst the darkness that was our childhood. She was the one who protected us, but we also protected her from him when his anger got out of control. But now, as I stand on shaky knees while she blames me for the family's problems, I realize that instead of looking to her to be the hero, I need to be my own champion. The one who was on my side growing up no longer is. Maybe she never was. All I know is I will not accept the liability for his problems any longer.

Suddenly, I have the urge to scream back at them and let my anger out to show the immense sadness I have for the 'loss' of my mother's support. Instead, I battle the adrenaline flowing through me as I keep my voice completely steady.

"I'm not destroying this family. I am trying to make myself a better person." There is strength in my tone that I don't recognize.

"How could you do this to your mother? She even brought you an Easter gift!" Dad yells, the features on his face arranged in outward disgust. Normally, his guilt trips would affect me, as it is his number one game against others—attack their empathy. With his opponent today, however, he has yet to realize that only apathy presents itself. I briefly glance at the bag in Mom's hand.

"That was very nice of her, but it still doesn't change the circumstances," I state objectively.

"Well, I'm definitely not giving it to her now," Mom responds sharply, wiping the tears from her eyes as she does. "You know what, let's go, Ken. We are clearly not welcome here."

She turns around, not even looking at me as does, and storms out the front door. I feel mixed emotions watching her leave. How many times have I defended her? How many times have I stood in front of her so he wouldn't physically hurt her? How many times has he berated her and made her feel like she was as small as a speck of dust? How—-HOW? How am I once again the problem of the family because I won't tolerate it any further? I blink my eyes a few times to clear the blurred edges of my vision as my mind tries to unwrap itself from a myriad of painful feelings hitting me at once.

"Do you know how many nights I have watched her cry because of you?" Venom is laced in Dad's voice as he interrupts my thoughts. I don't know if I want to laugh or cry at his words because I know that those nights are merely a tiny molehill in the mountain of terror that he, by himself, has created.

"I do not, but once again, you need to leave," I restate, more firmly this time. I can tell this battle has been won with my mother waiting in the car outside. He won't be here much longer. He takes a step forward, and I briefly feel a jolt through my chest, wondering if he is coming at me. He walks down to the family room grumbling '*Not her house anyway. Who does she think she is?*' I stay at the top of the short staircase and keep my eyes nervously trained on him. If he ends up going into Grandpa's office, I don't know what I'll do. Run in front of him first? He'll clearly know there is something to hide. Relief floods through me as he takes two cans of Pepsi from the refrigerator instead, a constant stream of angry grumbles never leaving his mouth before turning back around to come up the stairs. He doesn't say anything to me directly until he reaches the door, where he turns around and points a finger at me. "Since you don't seem to want parents in your life, then have it your way! I am done seeing *my* wife cry because of you!"

I say nothing in response, letting him have the last word with the hope that it'll make him finally leave.

"Who *are* you?" he says as he glares at me once more. I wait as he finally turns and slams the door behind him. Terrified that he will change his mind and come back to harass me more, I don't take my eyes off him for a second. Before he gets to the car, I see Terry's Suburban turning the corner. I let out a huge breath of relief knowing that even if Dad does stay, at least I don't have to fight alone anymore. Both Mary and Terry climb out moments after they park and make eye contact with Dad. He throws his arms up angrily and is shouting something to them. I can't hear what he is saying, but it's obviously awful.

It's only when I see the Suzuki pull out of the driveway that I notice my adrenaline coming down. It feels like a violent storm is passing through my knees, and I can barely stand. I make eye contact with Mary as she walks in the door, my feet still glued to the same spot in the foyer. Tremors are visibly going up and down my body so strongly now that I don't even try to mask it. I can't tell if I'm saddened, angry, or in disbelief at the delirium that is our family. The two camps may have been fighting all year, but it seems more real than ever now, as the line in the sand has officially been drawn by both parties.

There is no going back now.

MARY:

"Are you fucking proud of yourself, Mary Albrecht?! You have successfully weaseled your way in between Katie and her mother, you little bitch. I don't know how you can sleep at night." Ken slams the passenger door to the car, yelling at June, "GO NOW!" when he sees Terry exit our Suburban. The coward doesn't want to get in an altercation with Terry, knowing he will lose. Only the Albrechts put up with his shit. Until now.

We enter my dad's house to find Katie glued to one spot in the foyer, agitation evident by her flushed face. Terry and I encourage her to sit down, which she finally does downstairs.

"My mom... she blamed *me*. Her exact words were '*Look at what YOU are doing to this family.*'"

Katie chokes out the words, pulling her legs up and hugging herself into a human ball on the family room bench. I'm not used to seeing the usually confident and strong Katie so crushed. Especially by her mother. My protective instinct boils. I cannot fathom for even an instant why June would side with her deranged abuser over her own daughter.

I squat into a deep knee bend so that I am at eye level with Katie. Placing my hands on her tucked-up legs, I pronounce with a certainty that surprises even me, "You are the best thing that ever happened to this family, that's what you are doing." Terry makes his way up to the living room to talk to Stuart.

I realize just now how much I've come to love this brave young lady. Pride for knowing her brings tears to my eyes. We sit silently together for quite a while, Katie crying it out, my heart suffering from her pain. I know the agony of being blamed for something so blatantly not your fault by the person who is supposed to *always* have your back—your own mom. It cuts a hole in your spirit.

———

Later in the day I return to the hospital, surprised to find my dad slurring into the phone.

"Ken… I cannot… I'm too… tired. I don't want . . . to talk… about Katie".

He drops the phone and flops his head back on the pillow, shutting his eyes and emitting a long sigh.

"Daaad…" I can clearly make out Ken's disgusting whine despite the receiver being buried in the blankets.

The monitors go off, indicating his blood pressure and heart rate spiking. Nurses come rushing in, and I jump at the chance to grab the phone and set it in its cradle. Slipping out to the nurses' station, I resolutely put Ken on the blocked caller list, feeling a surge of empowerment as I do so. It hits me that I actually have rights at this moment; my dad is incapacitated, and I have health care power of attorney. This unfamiliar entitlement liberates me, and I march deliberately down to security and block Ken, not just from calling, but from the entire hospital. For once, for now, I have won.

————

The victory is fleeting, however, since we are barely in the front door upon my dad's discharge a few days later when we hear Ken's bellowing voice through the answering machine.

"You can't really think you can keep me away from my own daughter, Dad! You will regret it."

My weak, frail father slumps into his favorite recliner, folding his head into his hands. The doctors think he will make a full recovery, but not with this stress I'm afraid. There is simply no degree of empathy in this beast we call Ken. He just lost his mother, his father has had a stroke, and yet he still can only obsess about getting control, getting Katie back under his thumb, and being right. He has to win. A true sociopath. By the time I retrieve all of the messages, there are 37 threatening ones from Ken in three days. He's dangerously amped up.

Leaving my dad to rest, I go to the grocery store to stock his fridge. When I return just 30 minutes later, I find my dad in his den with the phone to his ear, head drooped, his other hand holding it up. From his bent over position, I can see the bones of his spine through his thin shirt and I am shocked by the vision of a very old man in front of me. My robust, strong, put-together, successful father is no longer here. My mom's death. His stroke. Ken. He has aged 10 years in a few months.

His voice cracks as he mumbles into the phone.

"Ken, I can't make Katie do what she doesn't want to do."

Inaudible yelling . . .

"No. I don't think Mary brainwashed her."

Did my dad just take my side?

The yelling magnifies and my dad crumbles further. I have to stop this, have to get Ken off the phone, have to help my dad. But if I am the one to intervene, I will make it worse. Stuart is the only other person here, though, and he never gets involved. Panic floods my system.

Suddenly, out of nowhere, an unfamiliar voice rips through the tense air. "God dammit! I can't take it!" Storming into my dad's den, Stuart tears the phone away.

"KEN. STOP. DAD IS DONE TALKING TO YOU FOR TODAY. HE NEEDS REST."

Who is this strong and confident man?

More shouts on the other end.

"I SAID STOP. YOU ARE DONE TALKING. I AM HANGING UP THE PHONE. DO NOT COME DOWN HERE. WE WILL CONTACT YOU WHEN WE ARE READY."

More shouts… then *slam*. The phone is on the receiver.

Never in my lifetime have I seen Stuart with a backbone, with authority, with a powerful sense of self.

———

For several days after, it is quiet. Katie, Stuart, my dad and I are connected as a united front blocking Ken. It's unfamiliar to be part of something bigger than his craziness. Is this how healthy families feel? Intertwined? Comfortable? Loved? I could get used to this. As I drive through Libertyville doing errands, gratitude warms my heart. I am happy Katie is here, in my life, and helping us. Perhaps we can come together after all.

The loud ringtone of my phone interrupts my sappy thoughts. When I see it's my dad calling, my hackles rise instinctively, until I remember that we are different with Ken now. I don't need to worry.

"Hi, Dad," I greet him cheerfully through the Bluetooth in the car. "How are you today?"

"Well…" my dad clears his throat, "Ken is on his way over here." His voice is still weak and I'm sure I must have not heard him correctly.

"What, Dad?" I remain cheerful but suddenly something feels ominous.

"His car broke down in Racine and he had it towed to Rouse's."

My body turns cold. The psychopath found an excuse to get back here. Rouse's Auto Repair is a local business right here in Libertyville. Racine is over 30 minutes away.

"He says he's walking over here right now." My dad coughs into the phone.

A knee-jerk reaction causes me to pull off the main road and park on a remote side street. Ken is here. In town. Walking these very streets right now. Stuck here without a car for who knows how long.

And he's incensed. I slink down in my car out of sight.

"He's faking, Dad." Desperation is evident in my voice. "Do you really believe his car broke down? He's trying to get to Katie. How is he going to get back to Wisconsin?" I'm screeching now.

"Well, I don't know, Mary. Even this becomes complicated." My dad sighs wearily. "Don't you think you are being a bit harsh?"

In an instant, it's all back. The insulting tone, the disdain for what I think, the degrading arrogance. The ridiculous maxim that it is *me* who is being harsh. I swallow hard, choking on disappointment.

"I'll call you back, Dad." I hang up before he can say anything else.

I realize I am practically hyperventilating. Only a few days without Ken's control of our family has begun to fill an almost insatiable hunger for peace. I am not ready go back into starvation while he gets stuffed with everything.

He is a parasite, that's what he is. I take out my phone and type in the word. Despite my anxiety, I smile at the absurdity as I stow away on the back roads of my hometown, hiding from my brother, reading dictionary.com.

PAR-A-SITE: NOUN

AN ORGANISM THAT LIVES IN OR ON ANOTHER
ORGANISM (ITS HOST) AND BENEFITS BY
DERIVING NUTRIENTS AT THE HOST'S EXPENSE.

That's him exactly. He sucks nutrients from us and has been away from his host too long. He is desperate, demented—a more aggressive parasite, I now fear.

Oh my God, he's going to win again.

The thought of Ken with my compromised dad for potentially several days is frightening. He is spiraling out of control—worse than I've ever witnessed. We have to get him out of Libertyville. If we don't, something very bad will happen.

I jump when the phone rings, practically hitting my head on the roof of the car. It's Stuart.

"Did you hear? He's back. He's coming here."

"I know, Stuart. It's bad. The stress is going to kill Dad. We have to get him out of town."

Just then, Ken's bellowing voice permeates the phone line as he storms into my dad's house, rage exploding so loud I have to remind myself that I'm more than a mile away.

"Where is she? I want to see my daughter! She is MYYYYY daughter, she belongs to me. You can't keep me from her!"

"Ken—I don't want you here. Especially when you act like this." My dad tries to sound strong but is still so shaky.

"I have noooooo fucking way to get home, Dad. Come on! My car broke down and you won't help me?"

"I don't believe you." Did my dad really say that?

"You don't believe me—YOU. DON'T. BELIEVE. YOUR. OWN. SON? What bullshit has Mary been feeding you?"

"This has nothing to do with Mary," Stuart shouts. There is a scuffling noise and the phone slams to the ground. I hear screaming from all three of them.

"Ken, I'm driving you home to Milwaukee. Get in the car. Let's go." Stuart sounds amazingly tough.

"No, Stuuuuuart…"

"YES, KEN!" The new Stuart from earlier in the week is back. "Or I will call the police. I mean it—DO NOT think I won't."

The police threat always scares Ken, the ultimate coward that he is. But he has to know you aren't bluffing. Stuart is more adamant than I have ever heard him sound in my life.

There are angry and inaudible words, then stomping, and the sound of a door opening and closing. My dad picks up the phone and says that Ken and Stuart have left. For the second time this week Stuart has intervened between my dad and Ken to protect us. A show of strength no one knew Stuart had, probably not even him. This *has* to be what healthy families do for each other—step up for what is right, no matter how hard.

Maybe there is hope for us still.

Chapter 20

KATIE:

As I pull off the highway that leads to South Milwaukee, the clouds are bright and fluffy and look brilliant in contrast to the blue sky behind them. It is Saturday afternoon, and the traffic wasn't bad, so I could relax and enjoy the ride. I have a One Direction CD playing because that always puts me in a good mood. I am early for my meeting. Eric and his girlfriend, Lisa, have been two of my best friends since high school. When Eric asked me to help pick out an engagement ring, it was an instant 'yes', even knowing I would have to drive back to South Milwaukee to do it. My parents won't suspect I am in the area, so it should be okay.

The drive into town is a familiar one. Businesses pass by me—Farm and Fleet, Culvers, and the Piggly Wiggly that is two blocks from my parents' house. All of them give me memories of home, or what it used to be. This place doesn't welcome me anymore. As I get closer to the street I grew up on, I can't help but have a strong curiosity about the house. I want to see it again, even if I just drive by. I wouldn't dare go inside, as Dad is likely on the couch, but to pass by on the way to Eric's house shouldn't be a problem, right? It's only a little out of the way. I continue to drive to the next intersection immediately following the Piggly Wiggly and wait for cars to pass before I make a right turn. Listening to the gentle rumble of the engine, my breath hitches in my throat. Stopped at the intersection, coming from the very direction in which I am turning, is a tan Suzuki. In that Suzuki are both of my parents.

I panic as I try to shield my face. I can't let them see me—not when I am this close to their house. I quickly make my right turn, and at the last minute, risk a glance as I pass them. Luckily, they are clearly not aware of their surroundings, especially not that their 23-year-old estranged daughter is a mere twenty feet from them. It has only been a couple weeks since Easter, but it feels like forever since I have seen them. I take in their expressions. Dad seems to be sporting his usual air of disgust. Mom's face holds a high level of distress, like she would rather be anywhere else but in a car with him. Though I can feel Mom's pain through the closed windows, resentment takes over. I don't know what I had expected, really. Maybe that she would be happy to be around him since she blatantly blamed me for everything a couple weeks ago? I guess I hoped that she was making this choice because she was happy with him, not because she felt like she was forced to do it. Seeing her now so miserable in the car with him angers and saddens me at the same time. How can she think I am worse than him?

I pass their car unnoticed and make my way to the street that was my home until a few months ago. In the midst of my hurt, anger, and confusion, I make a flash decision to do something a little risky. Parking on the street, slightly down the block from their house, I glance in the rear-view mirror for any sign of that Suzuki. When it looks clear, I hop out of my car and briskly walk towards their house, my eyes never leaving the end of the street that they disappeared from just minutes ago. I run up the driveway to the side door that leads into the kitchen. My pulse quickens as I insert my old key in the knob, surprised that they have not changed the locks. Since I have no idea where they were going, I'm terrified of when they could make their return. It could be any amount of time. I can't believe I am doing this.

I open the door and dart inside. The small yellow-tinted kitchen is cluttered as usual, so many piles on the table you can't even see the surface. I am hit with a scent that comes from a home that doesn't get proper cleaning and the smell of a man that doesn't either. For a long time, these vulgar senses brought association to 'home'. Not anymore.

I dart up the stairs and run past my sister's bedroom into mine. At first, everything seems to be exactly as I left it, stuff cluttered from the corners of the room and all the way across the floor. But then I notice several white plastic bags filled with piles of my clothes. I realize with a pang in my chest that they are stuffed into garbage bags as if they are about to be thrown out. Mom is getting rid of my things.

I try to ignore the hurt I feel from this. A part of me accepted when I left that I could no longer claim these possessions as my own, but I had hoped Mom would realize that I wasn't the problem. Her doing this, basically discarding any remnants of me, proves just the opposite. Tears well up at the base of my eyes, a drop hitting one of the garbage bags. This was something I wish I hadn't seen.

A car rushes by outside, and I quickly push down the emotions and start grabbing things that matter to me. I make a beeline for books, notebooks, and other paper-like things. After digging through the clutter, I find exactly what I was looking for—a stack of my childhood journals containing a lifetime of events in my own words. Clothes, shoes, and bags are just trivial—my memories are my life. Seeing that Mom is getting rid of my stuff, I fill my arms with all that I can carry, knowing very well that I only have one shot.

I continue picking up a few more things—a couple of books, an extra pair of socks and shoes. The thought briefly crosses my mind to take the bags of my clothes that Mom ever so kindly packed up, but I decide against it as then she would know someone has been here. I wish I could spend more time, but my nerves are escalating. Based on their hateful texts and bagging up of my things, they would consider me an intruder in their house. And yet they probably wouldn't let me leave.

A toppled-over picture on one of the dressers catches my attention. I swallow hard as I see it's the three of us—Mom and Dad with me standing between them. We are all smiling. I have a swim cap and t-shirt on since it is Parents' Night during my senior year of high school swim team. I remember cringing even then, having to stand so close to Dad, not knowing at the time that he would become way more deranged and disheveled once the drugs took their toll. I don't know what compels me to do it, but I grab the photograph off the dresser and add it to the pile in my arms.

I run back through the upper landing, trying not to drop even one of the mismatched items, and hurry down the stairs. As I approach the side door through the kitchen, I hear a rumble of a car engine nearby. I halt in my exact spot and feel my heart hammering wildly.

Slowly approaching the door, I peel open the curtains just enough to peek outside. My eyes scan the driveway and take in its emptiness, realizing that for at least another moment, I am safe. However, because of the angle of the house, I cannot see the end of the driveway if a car is turning into it. I realize I have no choice.

Taking a deep breath, I open the door, jam it shut with my body, and dart behind the bush on the side of the house. When it seems like the coast is clear, I turn and sprint towards my car down the block without looking back. It is not until I drive several streets away that I feel my body release the extraordinary amount of tension it had been holding. I pull over and close my eyes.

'Look at what you are doing to this family'.

I can still hear Mom's voice reverberating in my ears. Now that the adrenaline is waning, sadness creeps over me instead. I can't believe that this is where my life has gone, feeling so unsafe around my parents that I have to wait until they are gone and sneak into their house. Their daughter is trying to do the right thing for herself and is shunned because of it. This is my reality now.

I still have to meet my friend Eric. I try my best to pull myself together, once again pretending that everything is okay. Pulling out of the neighborhood with a final gasp of pain, I don't know if I will ever be back.

Chapter 21

Mary:

I am a nervous wreck. I started drinking at noon to plow through the sadness that comes with what we have to do today. It is the second day of May and the ground is thawed, so it's time to put my mom's ashes in the memorial garden plot. This is the first time the whole family has been together since the intervention, and I haven't seen Ken since Easter. Katie's relationship with her parents is on the verge of shattering into even more pieces than it already is in. Eventually there will be no chance of repair, and how today plays out is critical.

My whole body is on fire as I ride in the passenger seat of our Suburban on the way to the church. The sun is beating through the glass, and the heat from it is suffocating. I roll down the window, sticking my entire head and upper body out to try to cool down.

"You okay?" Terry calmly checks in on me knowing that I totally am *not*.

"I can't do this. I don't want to see him. And I don't want to face my mom's death again."

"Let's just get it over with," Katie says from the back seat, as she has chosen to arrive with us for reinforcements.

As we enter the church garden, I see that Ken and June have already arrived. I look at June for any sign of warmth, but there is only ice in her eyes. Ken won't acknowledge me, but his anger radiates out of every pore as he takes his position in the half circle we have formed around the burial plot. The tension hits so hard I immediately become light-headed and the atmosphere begins to buzz around me.

The pastor begins with a prayer. We barely say 'Amen' when Ken shifts his stance, sighing and grunting simultaneously.

"Can I say something?" His words are garbled.

The pastor is polite but firm when he explains that this isn't the funeral and we don't have eulogies now.

Ken ignores him. "My mother was the symbol of forgiveness and the most fantastic lady I've ever met…" He is swaying now, and the slurring becomes more pronounced. No one dares to breathe as the pastor allows him to continue. "She would be so disappointed in our family…" He stops as he stumbles backward, June catching his arm.

"Ken, this isn't the time," she whisper-yells.

"She would be sooo sad…"

"Ken, stop." This time it's my dad. "Let the pastor continue."

Ken digs in for more. "Our family is broken, and we all know how much this would hurt Grandma, the most beautiful person who loved *all* of her grandchildren, despite what they do wrong."

Katie and I exchange knowing glances. He is going for the jugular now.

"Dad. STOP." Now it's Josh. He usually can get through to Ken.

There is palpable silence as we all wait for the reaction from the simmering volcano in front of us. He is groaning as he breathes.

"I will stop if I can be the one to lower the urn in the ground." His usual bargaining now.

"Your father should do that, Ken." The pastor is adamant.

"I want to do it. She is *my* mother." Ken glares so harshly at the pastor I am worried he will launch a physical attack.

"But he is her spouse. That's what she would want, I'm sure." The pastor's tone is shifting to impatience.

"It's okay," my dad concedes. "You can do it, Ken. I know your love for your mother was special."

I gasp louder than I intended and Terry takes my hand, squeezing it to silence me from the reaction that is clearly at my lips. I close my eyes in defeat.

The sound of Ken's movement alerts me to open my eyes. He is staggering toward the hole in the ground with my mom's ashes in hand. As he trips on nothing, I envision the entire contents of the urn flying out into the wind, symbolically letting my mom get lost from us forever.

"Let me help, Ken." My dad steps in.

"Stay away from me! She is *my* mother…" Ken hisses.

As he struggles to kneel down and put the urn in the hole, I look at his pathetically large body and the back of his greasy head bowed over the hole, and I suddenly feel sorry for this messed up person in front of us desperately trying to hang on to our mom for just a moment longer. I back out of the circle and take a seat on a nearby bench.

Absorbing the group in front of me, I see tense and disconnected people. Sadness overwhelms me for what we are. Not sadness because of Katie's actions but for the void of what was not done to put an end to Ken's misery in the form of help. For his sake as well as ours. Just trying to get through the day and 'keeping the peace' for decades has led to this tortured being hunched over on the ground, hugging his mother's urn to his body, filled with grief.

We ceremoniously take turns scooping dirt into the hole, slowly burying my mom's remains. As we hand the shovel to one another there is no eye contact, no compassion, and no support. We are a bunch of robots pretending to be a unit just to do the right thing for my mom. The coldness is evident even on this warm day, and I wonder how we will ever repair what this so-called family has become.

As we walk back to our cars, I take one look back at the memorial garden and see Ken lingering longer than any of us. A mixture of pity and fear pervades my mind as I ponder what will become of him without my mom. I wish to console him or somehow use this tragedy to get closer to him. Despite the abuse, I actually do feel this way right now. Maybe we can bond over this disabling grief. Perhaps I can have an older brother in at least some way that the title always seemed it should be.

We gather at my dad's house to decompress before our planned dinner out at my mom's favorite restaurant. Since the day is still so beautiful, we eventually end up outside, scattered on the front porch and lawn. I see June over in the driveway and suggest to Katie that we go say hello. Katie agrees reluctantly. A chill runs up my spine as we approach her stiff and defensive body, and I try to break the ice by saying that Katie misses her. It is as if a hot waterfall pours over June, melting the coldness as she lunges toward Katie and pulls her into a suffocating embrace. Katie stands completely still, her arms hanging at her sides.

"Mom. Mom. Mom. We are not okay." Katie wiggles her way out of the hug and steps back, escaping into the house.

Feeling awkward, I remain with June, hoping to assuage her sadness from her daughter's distance and per-haps counsel her on how to bridge the gap. Instead, anger spews from her mouth.

"Katie and Ken are a lot alike."

I'm stunned beyond speechless. Katie and Ken are a lot alike? It's as if she just spoke a foreign language.

Apparently, my shock is evident because June continues discharging her venom.

"They both hold onto grudges way longer than is healthy. They both want to have the last word and neither one will budge. I can't take having two of them in my life."

My head explodes.

SO YOU CHOOSE YOUR ABUSIVE MENTALLY ILL HUSBAND OVER YOUR CHILD? THE ONE WHO LIES AND CHEATS AND PHYSICALLY HURTS YOU? THE ONE WHO STEALS MONEY AND USES IT FOR DRUGS? THE ONE YOU CAN'T STAND TO BE WITH, EVEN ADMITTING THAT YOU GOT A SECOND JOB TO GET AWAY FROM HIM? NOT TO MENTION THE OBVIOUS TRUTH THAT KATIE IS NOOOOTTTTHHHHHING LIKE HER FATHER! WHAT'S WRONG WITH YOU, WOMAN? DO YOU EVEN KNOW YOUR DAUGHTER AT ALL?

"Mary? Mary?" I barely hear June's voice over the lightning in my brain.

"You seemed to have disappeared." It's only then that I realize that none of my words were voiced out loud. They were only fireworks in my mind. I now wonder why I didn't say them to her. Am I like the rest after all—trying to keep the peace?

I am jolted out of my stupor when I hear Ken's badgering voice directed toward Katie. I glance up to the porch to see Ken waddling toward her where she sits on the swing, yelling indecipherable words. Katie bolts off the other side of the porch, literally running away from him.

She stops at the edge of the front lawn, arms folded tight across her, shoulders hunched, distress clear in her eyes.

Now I can hear Ken. We all can, including any neighbors.

"Come on, Katie! This is about your mother! I can't believe you would be so mean to not come to Mother's Day! Come on, Katie, just say you'll come. Please? Please? It's for your *mother* for God's sake…" His voice is now begging.

"Dad… just stop… I can't do this right now…" Katie takes a couple of steps closer to her car.

Ken's voice turns to the familiar whiny yelling. "Just come next week, Katie. Just say you'll come. Not for me but for your mother. Come on, Katie!" He is spiraling from lack of control as Katie puts her hand on her car door.

"I'm sorry. I just can't do this." She looks over to me as I've now placed myself about halfway between her and Ken.

"Go," I say. "I get it."

She barely closes the driver door before she lurches into gear and peels away, fleeing around the corner and out of sight.

I had envisioned we would tell warm stories about my mom and share in the sadness for at least this one day. What a foolish thought to think it would be any different.

CHAPTER 22

MARY:

My head is glued to the pillow. I try to lift it, but it screams out in pain. Looking up at the ceiling, I blink several times to clear my blurred vision. I cried myself to sleep last night. Again.

I miss my mom. We didn't even talk about her yesterday at *her* memorial. It was all about Ken. Again.

My heart hurts as I roll over. The memorial should have brought peace, closure, togetherness—anything else than what really happened. We are more disconnected than ever, barely holding on to even a chance to make it better. This is what my mom left us with and I wonder if she can see it now, in Heaven, in a place where she doesn't have to pretend anymore. It remains unclear as to whether her death has made Ken worse or if it's just that there is no one to cover up the extent of his depravity anymore. What I have witnessed in the past several months is shocking even to me, the one who was so very abused by him. I simply cannot comprehend how anyone can think he is okay, that his treatment of others and of himself is remotely normal. It is appalling what this family will tolerate.

Ken's sinister voice from yesterday swarms all around me. I pull the covers over my head to hide, instantly throwing them off when his bloated face haunts my vision, even with my eyes closed. He is evil. He will do anything to be the center, the dictator, the tyrant. He even tried to control my mom's farewell. Revulsion swallows me up as I remember.

*****

"Sorry about your mom's cancer being back." I'm on the phone with my uncle Bob, my mom's youngest brother in northern Wisconsin. "But that's not why I called. Your idiot asshole of a brother has been calling everyone up here demanding we come down to your folks' house on December 14 for a surprise Packers party for your mom. But we are not to tell you or June that we are doing this. He is manipulating us with lines like, 'She doesn't have long to live' and 'It's probably the last chance for you to see her'."

"A goodbye party?" I whisper weakly.

"Yup. What a selfish bastard." Bob's words are laced with disgust. "Some of the people he called didn't even know her cancer was back."

My mom wouldn't want this. Even if she were healthy, she would never ask her relatives who live over 300 miles away to drive down in winter right before Christmas. And she is so very sick. The cancer is burning her up.

Bob continues, "Who the hell does he think is going to pay for the party anyway? He is so out of touch he might as well be on the moon, for Pete's sake. I can just see us all showing up at your mum's front door and then what? Stupid Kenny makes us goddamn hot dogs? While we sit around and stare at a dying lady? I swear, Mary, after your mother passes, I will be fine if I never see or hear from that loser again."

"Shit, Bob. Who else do you think he called?"

"He said he went through your mom's card file."

FUCK. That's hundreds of people.

———

Over the next several days my phone does not stop ringing.

'Is she really terminal?" Yes.

'A month to live?' Hopefully a few.

'Why didn't she tell me herself?' She's been very sick. It's happening fast.

'Would she really want us there?' No.

———

My mom slumps in her wheelchair in the hospital room when I tell her about the party. She plants her face in her hands, saying nothing. I know she is embarrassed that he did this, but of course she will not admit it. I don't bother to push her to say so because I cannot and will not allow Ken to cause me to hurt her, despite the fact that it is her rose-colored view of him that hurt me for so many years. Instead I tell her I have fixed the problem. Nobody is coming in December. We sit in silence in the stark hospital room, our hearts bleeding out for so many reasons.

*****

It must have been horrible being his mother. She would do anything to keep his illness a secret, as if it sickened her to have birthed a person like him. Now, she is gone, and we are stuck with the madness while she rests. Resentment duels with my sadness. She covered it all up, even until the very end. Even when it literally caused her physical pain.

*****

I go to the usual place on the shelf and pull down the box of medicine at my parents' house. It's been two months since my mom's terminal diagnosis and I sense that the end is rapidly approaching. I now give her morphine shots twice a day for the excruciating pain from the tumors pressing on her spine. I pull a syringe out of the special bag they are stored in, counting the remaining ones in the process. Morphine is a controlled substance and I want to be sure she has enough until the end of the month, when she can get more. I kiss her goodbye with the commitment to return at the end of the day like always.

When I return that evening, I cannot find the bag of morphine. I frantically dump the medicine box out and run my hands through the dozens of pill bottles, as if the bag could hide under them. I search the shelf the box was on, as well as all the other shelves. I plop down on the floor to see underneath the cabinet. There is no bag.

"Did you do something with the bag of morphine, Mom?"

"No, why?" She barely looks up from her magazine.

"It's not in the box where we always keep it." I can feel panic in my words.

"Well, I can't imagine what happened to it, Mary. You're the one to last see it. What did you do with it?"

"Mom. I put it back this morning. I'm sure of it."

"What's going on?" My dad emerges from the den.

"Mary lost the morphine," my mom states emphatically.

"I did NOT lose the morphine, Mom." I order myself to remain calm despite the accusatory words. "So nobody touched this box while I was gone?"

"Well, I had Ken get it down for me so I could take a Tylenol," she admits.

My blood turns cold. "Ken was here?"

"Yes, he was here for a couple of hours this morning." Does she really think that wasn't important to mention before?

"Mom… HE took your morphine. Don't you see? Why would you let a drug addict handle your box of prescriptions?"

"He wouldn't do that, Mary." Her condescending voice is back.

"Mom, the morphine was here this morning. He came and went before I returned. No one else was here, right? AND you asked him to hand you the box. And now the bag is gone. Come on, Mom!"

"I guess I don't know," she sighs. "I'm too tired for this."

"I'm calling Ken." My dad actually sounds angry.

"Just forget it, Arlyn. I'll be okay without it." She is always the martyr when it comes to Ken.

"No, you won't, Mom," I say loudly—desperately.

"He says Terry's guys must have taken it," my dad announces after hanging up the call with Ken.

"They weren't here today," I state bluntly.

"You sure you saw it this morning, Mary?" My mom seems delirious.

"I used it this morning, Mom! I gave you a shot." I am shouting now.

Silence.

And then the text from HIM.

Ken: Stealing my mom's morphine, Mary? Really? You blame me for everything. You are seriously messed up. I don't hate you. I feel sorry for you.

*****

He stole his dying mother's morphine and she let it go. She would rather live in unbearable pain than expose his twistedness. She couldn't get any more syringes for over 10 days until the end of the month. During this time, she suffered miserably at the hands of her son and then went into the hospital for the last time.

She died two weeks later.

CHAPTER 23

MARY:

We sit here mostly in silence, tension thickening the room. June is trying to make small talk with my dad since it is Father's Day. Stuart is rocking in the swivel chair talking to himself as usual. And then there is Ken. His yellowing undershirt has the sleeves cut out so deep that you can see the ripples of fat down to his waist from the arm holes. He lumbered in with old swim trunks on—barely. His butt crack was fully exposed, as it often is. He plopped that very butt crack down on the couch where he now remains. No eye contact, no words, just grunt-like sighs. He has socks on, again barely. Three toes with unsightly long and jagged toenails are exposed through a huge hole on one foot. The other foot exposes a crusty heel. As for June, it is obvious that she does not want to include me in her conversation by her posture, showing only her profile with one hand propping up her head so none of her features are exposed to me.

I study Ken at length, as he now has part of a blanket on his tilted-back head, covering his eyes. His face is bloated, blotchy, and discolored. His stomach looks like a watermelon has grown inside. His breathing is labored, chest rising and falling rapidly. This has to be more than missing Katie on Father's Day. It seems to me his body is very distressed. But knowing Ken, he will outlive us all. Stuart and I say he is too evil to die because then he could not torture us. I cannot help but feel sorry for this broken beast in front of me. My brother. Ken. Bro-Ken. My bro, Ken, is broken. I smile at my clever play on words. Not only is he broken himself, he breaks apart each of us individually, and collectively as a family. In the past, when he still had good sides that presented, I would reverse his name when the ugliness came out. 'Nek is back' I would write in my journals. No one knew this nickname for him at the time. Now only Katie shares this information. We both call him Nek often now since he is *always* angry and horrible.

As my thoughts continue to wander in this uncomfortable, stifling room, I smirk when I put the two words together. Broken Nek. Hilariously tragic and tragically hilarious in that this is truly who he is. He strangles our family; he certainly strangles me. He has twisted my head up to the point that my neck could snap at any time. A vision now surfaces of me being the one to break his neck first, of him lying there, still my bro, Ken, who is broken, who is Broken Nek, but this time he is truly dead, his head at a right angle to his body, ending his threatening hold over all of us once and for all.

So this is what forgiveness leads to? Sitting here with this miserable and despondent human being like it is perfectly natural? Forgiveness was my mom's main argument. 'I choose forgiveness, Mary' was her recurring mantra when I begged her for change.

'But forgiving him means allowing him to hurt us, Mom. And ultimately it's hurting him, too.'

'Sounds like your psychologist babble speak, Mary. I don't need psychology. I have God.' Her tone is cutting, diminishing me.

'Well then how about talking to your pastor about helping Ken?' I already know the answer by her expression.

'I would *never* share this with my pastor. And don't you ever try that again.'

*****

Sitting in a new member meeting at my parent's church as a 35-year-old woman feels ridiculous. I'm in a difficult place in my marriage and succumbed to my mom's pressure to try to include God more systematically in my life. The other people in this meeting seem like they fit here. Allison and Ben, a newlywed couple who cannot speak without seeking adoring affirmation from each other. The older couple who have no prob-

lem bragging about their ultra-successful children and perfect grandchildren. The "pretty" couple with the blond, tan, ultra-coiffed wife wearing diamonds that blind accompanied by her handsome husband in a pristine suit and designer shoes.

And me. Frumpy and useless with nothing to offer except that I'm my parents' child. I ride on their coattails for the rest of the hour, no identity except that I'm an Albrecht, which in this church goes a long way.

As the meeting adjourns, the pastor approaches me.

"I just love your parents, Mary."

Of course, you do, I think cynically as I put on my best fake smile. They give loads of money AND volunteer for practically every committee.

"They are wonderful people. And your mom is always talking about your older brother. What a fabulous family he has. He sounds like a fantastic father. You are so lucky to have a family like this." The pastor is practically gushing.

The words slice my skin. Something snaps in my brain, and hostility involuntarily spews from my mouth.

"Actually, my older brother is a mess. He's an addict, a liar, a thief, and an abuser. He is diseased. My parents try to keep it hidden. They even pay him to go away. Can you please help us?"

Silence. He is looking at me like I just spoke a foreign language. His eyes grow cold, his jaw tightens, and he folds his arms across his front.

Am I imagining his body language? Surely a man of God is willing to care for all types.

"Please, will you help?" My voice rises an octave and I now sound like a little girl.

Tension pours into the room like a torrential rain. He is speaking now, but the words are garbled. Something about getting back to me? He smiles and scurries from the room.

I run into the bathroom, lock myself in the closest stall, and sink down onto the toilet fully clothed. Holding my hands to my ears, I start rocking back and forth. I'm going to be in such trouble with my parents. I have broken the family contract of secrecy and surely will be sentenced.

I thought I had learned my lesson when I was 13. The memory invades the entire stall as I continue to hide from my crimes of honesty:

> My head is spinning, I'm so depressed, I can't focus on school. Is this what it's like to be a teenager? I feel like I'm underwater in a dirty lake, and I keep sinking further down no matter how hard I try to crawl up. I'm desperate for air, to the point of losing consciousness

soon. I don't even remember how I got here but I'm sitting in the school social worker's office crying and gasping. It all comes spilling out... my life at home is unbearable, Ken is out of control, my dad is gone working all the time, my mom says I'm the problem... that I'm too hard on Ken.

"I can't take it anymore." Saliva gets stuck in my throat. "No one believes me. No one will help me."

"I can help you, Mary," the social worker says compassionately.

I look at her through my swollen eyes and stare. The ticking of the clock is all I hear. Did someone just say they would help?

She says she will call my parents. She will defend me. She will make it better.

Suddenly I can breathe again.

———

It is early evening and I have been sleeping since I got home from school, trying to escape from the emotions of the day. I'm in my typical hiding spot in my room, where most of the time Ken doesn't bother me. But the door bursts open and my mom towers over me, red face and seething eyes.

"How dare you air our family troubles to that social worker bitch!"

I rub my eyes and prop up against the headboard. "What are you talk... oh, did she call already?"

"That snippy ignorant voice trying to tell me how to raise MY family. How could you, Mary?"

"She says Ken needs help, Mom. Can we please help him?"

"Clearly YOU are the one who needs help, or you wouldn't have ended up in a social worker's office." She is really angry at me.

"Yes, I need help trying to get help for Ken," I try to reason.

"Ken needs love. Love will transcend. You need to love him, Mary." It comes out as an order.

"Seems to me I am the one loving him by trying to get him help." I'm probably pushing it too far, but I can't seem to stop myself.

"There you go again with your psychological crap. God is enough for me and God wants me to forgive." My mom's words stab at my heart.

"But doesn't God also want sick people to get help? And didn't God create psychologists?" I am standing now, with my hands on my hips, inches away from my mom.

"Well, you just have all the answers in that 13-year-old brain of yours, huh? The God model doesn't place boundaries on people, Mary." She is talking down to me more than ever.

"What?! How about the Ten Commandments?" I won't give up the fight.

Until I do.

———

Somehow the social worker went away. She told me she was busy and couldn't see me anymore. She looked at me like I was out of my mind.

———

And now the pastor just looked at me the same way.

*****

I blink back the tears that nobody sees trickling down my face. I'm remembering way too much since Katie moved here. It's really all I think about now. I am lost in this evil place again, barely holding on to my current identity. Ken was awful, but my parents never helped me, never defended me, never heard me. And he didn't get the help he so desperately needed.

So here we sit on the first Father's Day since my mom's death and this is the carnage we are left with. Five family members sitting in the same room, physically close to each other but not together, hatred hanging in the air, minimal conversation between June and my dad, and two brothers who don't even see me. One talking to himself. The other not talking at all.

So much for forgiveness.

CHAPTER 24

KATIE:

It's Fourth of July weekend, the celebration of our nation's independence. I have been seeing a lot of posts on Facebook of my friends celebrating in their summer clothes and lounging around their lake houses. They are probably grilling hot dogs and brats, letting the sun cook their skin to a pleasant golden brown, or an unavoidable lobster red. This weekend is meant to represent relaxation—a celebration of freedom is best when you're basking in it, right?

As I drive through Libertyville, I look over at the passenger seat at my backpack and purse, making sure I still have both since I don't know how long my parents will be there tonight. I have a new lock on my bedroom door, thanks to Terry installing it last week, so at least Dad won't be rifling through my belongings again. He claims he is coming down 'for Mary's birthday'. It's such a load of bull.

Based on what Mary has told me in the few months since I have lived here, and his general level of manipulation, the notion that he just wants to come down to celebrate with her couldn't be further from the truth.

A twinge of sadness hits me as I think about Mary's birthday today. I want to do something for her, or at the very least spend time with her. But *Nek,* as Mary and I so 'affectionately' call him now, is doing that instead. A scenario that *none* of us want. I took enough things for overnight just in case Grandpa can't get him to leave this time. Notes of bitterness stream their way through me that this is my weekly routine.

I haven't seen either of my parents since Grandma's memorial back in May. I know it's not right to continue staying at Grandpa's house when I refuse to talk to his son, and I desperately would like to leave because of that. The more I try to fade into the background, the more I'm driving a wedge in this family. I wish I had more than a couple part-time jobs so that I could afford to move out. Leaving Libertyville would be sad, though, as Mary has become the family member I never knew I always wanted. It's hard to walk away from something like that.

As I turn the corner onto the street of the Fitness Loft, "Born in the USA" by Bruce Springsteen comes on the radio. My eyes dart with a jolt to the 101.9 on my car's dashboard as if to blame those digital numbers for reminding me. It takes me a second to register that it's only playing because it's July 3, and radio stations like to show off their exaggerated sense of patriotism around this time.

'No one is more talented than the BOSS', Nek would say growing up because Bruce has always been his favorite singer. He typically said it as he laughed in my face whenever I took interest in a different band. It was his form of 'light-hearted teasing' and probably one of his few harmless habits. But in my angsty teenage years, I hated it.

'Green Day is pretty darn good though, Dad,' I would argue with confidence.

We'd go back and forth like this several times in a year, and I always took the bait. He was good at throwing out the reel and fishing for a big argument. To an outsider, this particular instance probably looked like gentle banter between a father and daughter, but it felt like never-ending salt being poured into countless wounds on my body. Not only was he trying to 'one up' my interests, but he was also minimizing the pain and worry we felt every time we heard Springsteen play. Springsteen may be talented, and hell, it's not his fault that his music leaves a bitter taste in my mouth, but with it playing every time Dad drank growing up, it's hard not to feel my muscles tense up every time one of those songs comes on.

I pull into the lot of the Loft, grateful that Mary has offered it to me as a 'hang out' in the times Nek comes to Libertyville. He is not welcome at Mary's place of business; she has made that clear with the restraining orders through the years. The song ends, and my muscles relax as I kill the ignition. I realize that while my friends are celebrating the freedom of our nation, I am celebrating the 'freedom' from my manipulative father. The price I pay? Separation from the rest of my family. Our founders knew it best when separating our country from England; the cost of freedom can be so high that you will never truly be free.

*****

Mom, Josh, Sandra, and I exit the car and head toward the house. We have just gotten back from Josh's high school fresh-man basketball game. Dad stayed behind 'for some reason'. We hear that very reason blasting through the walls: Bruce Springsteen, Born in the USA.

That is our warning. Every time he plays Springsteen, we know there is a storm brewing.

I can see my grimace mirrored on my family's faces. We brace ourselves and open the side door that leads into the kitchen. The music instantly surrounds me and the bass echoes through my entire body as the barrier of the door disappears. I am the first one in the house and half expect to see him standing there waiting for all of us to come home. Instead, I find something much more terrifying.

I gasp as I see Mom's largest butcher knife standing straight up with the blade stuck in the kitchen table. I catch the attention of the others and they gaze past me to see what is happening. The color seems to drain from their faces as we all look at one another, silently asking the same question.

What is he planning on doing with that?

We hesitantly step into the kitchen and do not see Dad. However, when Mom walks past me toward the knife, he turns the corner from the hallway at the very same moment. The first thing I notice is how shiny and red he looks. He typically has a natural sheen of oil on his skin due to his lack of hygiene, but it especially comes out when he has been drinking. And sure enough, when I look down, the beer bottle in his hand is almost empty. Chances are, that is not his first one.

"What is this?" Mom asks, referring to the knife.

"It's a knife," Dad replies simply, as if it deserves no other explanation. He is standing in the doorway not coming any closer to us. This makes me feel more nervous than if he were to charge at us, since I'm not sure what is coming next.

"Well, why is it in the table?" Mom presses further. She sounds strong in her voice, but I can tell she is nervous by the way her upper lip trembles.

"It seemed like a good place to me," he says calmly. Again, his voice is eerily nonchalant.

"You can't do things like this. You are just trying to scare us," Mom says as she plucks the knife out of the table and puts it back in the drawer.

The yelling starts after that. I think Mom senses that we kids are scared even though we are contributing to the shouting match. So when he retreats to the bathroom, she grabs the house phone and hands it to me while telling us all to go into Josh's room. It is the only room that still has a lock on it since Dad has destroyed every other door on the first floor, some completely ripped from the hinges.

"Mom, should I call the police?" I ask her as we lock the door behind us. I still have the phone in my hands.

Before she can answer, the footsteps come near again and the door handle begins to jiggle. When he can't get in, the pounding starts.

"JUNE! LET ME IN RIGHT NOW. HOW DARE YOU KEEP MY KIDS FROM ME!" His voice bellows through the door.

I look at Mom and this time hold up the phone to indicate silently what I need permission to do. But she shakes her head and whispers, "Not yet. He should pass out soon."

We continue to wait behind that locked door, still not calling the cops. I start to envision what could happen. I start to actually see Dad walking down the hall slowly with the blade in his hand just like all the horror movies I have watched. I can visualize it clearly until I shudder and force myself to remember that it hasn't happened . . . yet. More yelling comes from the other side of the door, interrupting my thoughts. Mom tells him that she doesn't feel safe with him putting a knife in the table.

"I wasn't going to do anything with it. C'mon, June, do you really think I would hurt my kids? What's the matter with you!" he bellows through the door. But he seems to back away for some reason. Probably to go get another beer. This is all a game to him.

We begin our waiting game for him to pass out. Every so often he walks away for five minutes, but he always comes back. The fear lessens and annoyance takes over, as it usually does, but Mom doesn't let us out of the room. We go through this same cycle every time he drinks. Sometimes he becomes violent, and other times he just screams at us relentlessly. We never know which angry man we are going to get. When he is not howling, he comes back to tell of his disgust with us and the world. We don't mind this as much since it's not as bad as when he is physically violent with Mom. The insults roll off our skin like water droplets and eventually evaporate. But this time we stay behind this door, because it is the first time he has tried to scare us with a knife.

It's the same old lines over and over again. 'Your mother has brainwashed you to hate your father', he says to us kids. We argue back that he is the one trying to brainwash all of us.

Mom is a saint, after all. We may not get along all the time, but she brightens up the darkness we endure daily.

Dad always says that hate is a very strong word and should never be used on anyone. It's ironic because he doesn't seem to know the torture he gives to people or the hatred he possesses. He doesn't seem to remember that while he is getting drunk and listening to Springsteen, we are going through hell. Right now is a perfect example; all of the people that he supposedly 'loves' are hiding from him behind a locked door.

I am sick of feeling scared. I'm sick of feeling hurt, cautious, or angry. Whenever he is not raging, we walk on eggshells to prevent anything from escalating. We think that we have an ounce of control in this, but we don't. He demands control over us and stops at nothing to get it.

There has to be a better life than this. If hate is as strong of a word as Dad says it is, then I truly hate my father.

The pounding starts up again and the yelling increases in volume. As much as we all thought he would pass out, he seems to be doing the opposite, his energy levels ramping up. The door suddenly shakes violently and there is barely any time to register what is happening before it breaks open right before our eyes. He has broken down the other doors, and now he got to the very last one. He stands in the doorway in a fury, and our fear multiplies more than ever.

MARY:

I am 51 years old today and don't recognize my life. Nek is constantly harassing me, I am caring for my dad on a daily basis, and we moved into a new house two days ago. I ache for the old days, before cancer and stroke and Katie, though Katie herself is a bright spot. But this is too much. I want to hide from the world. It seems like my birthday, the first one without my mom, should be a day to take care of me. Yet Ken is trying to use it as a way to get to Katie through me. He and June are coming down to make me a birthday dinner. My dad pressured me to spend the evening with them, even though I told him I am very tired and could use a day to myself. He called me selfish for say-ing this, Nek's main verbal weapon against me, the word that makes my ears bleed. But this time it came from my father's mouth. I am disgusted by this family.

The drive over to my dad's house is painfully fast, so I go around the block and pull out of the subdivision. I can't believe I agreed to this. Terry is so mad I did that he is not joining me until later. Pulling into a parking lot near my childhood home, I turn on the radio and try to prepare myself mentally for what is ahead of me. Scrolling through the stations I land on 101.9 FM, recline my seat, and close my eyes. I wish I could spend the day with Katie instead. She is on her way over to the Loft right now to avoid her parents like she does every week. Every ounce of me wants to blow off the birthday dinner and go there. Katie has become the one family member who treats me the way I always thought families would. I had stopped hoping for that long ago. But now that I have the sweet surprise of my niece who gets me, gets all of it, I never want to be without it again.

The powerful introduction of "Born in the USA" by Bruce Springsteen causes me to jolt upright and open my eyes. Is this a cruel joke? Here I am trying to escape from Nek for a few minutes longer and his favorite artist, the one he is absolutely obsessed with, invades my private space. I haven't heard this song in years, since listening to "The Boss" has been ruined by association to that horrible person lurking just blocks away. I shudder when I think that he could be so super-humanly skilled at getting to me that he can control what's on the radio.

I roll my eyes at my stupidity when I realize that this song is playing because it's Fourth of July weekend. It's not Nek coming through the radio. Get a grip, Mary; I slap my cheeks to help focus. It's too bad that Springsteen evokes such negativity. For me it's even worse now since Katie shared her story about the knife. I have lived through what Katie has, yet it still shocks me to hear of the brutality in someone else's words. I've tried to help Katie remember what happened on that terrifying day when he bust down the bedroom door, but she draws a complete blank, probably needing to block it out for mental health. My head spins when I consider the possibilities.

I often compare Nek to the herpes virus. A condition that is gross and painful, that cycles between flare-ups and dormancy but is never gone because there is no cure. I am scarred from this virus, since I was its main residence. I sense another flare-up on its way at tonight's dinner. I sigh in defeat. I simply do not, never have had, and won't ever have any rights when it comes to Ken. They want me to robotically sacrifice my needs and agree to do exactly what I *don't* want to do, even though they abandoned me on this very day for years.

*****

"I can't believe I will be 40 in a few months, Mom." We are having one of our monthly lunches out. *"You are right—time goes faster as you get older."*

"Speaking of your 40th, Mary, we have booked a cabin up in Saint Germaine, Wisconsin, right on Little Saint Germaine Lake for the week over the Fourth of July. There's plenty of room for you to come."

"That's great, Mom! A perfect 40th birthday gift. Is that the idea?"

"Well… Ken called and asked if we could do this." My mom is trying to sound casual.

My fork crashes to the plate. *"Ken is involved?"*

"He said if we would book a cabin then he would be willing to do a family vacation. The best time to get everyone together is over the Fourth of July because then June won't have to take as many vacation days."

"Ken is 'willing' to do a family vacation, Mom? What does that mean? Like he's gracing you with his family as long as you do the buying?"

"Now, Mary, that's a little harsh. I think it's nice."

"I really don't want to vacation with Ken. Especially over my 40th birthday."

"I thought you'd say that."

"Then why did you book it if you knew I wouldn't come?"

"I just told you, because that's the best time for June."

"But don't you think you should have checked with me since it's my birthday week?" I'm hoping for some consolation.

"I told you there is plenty of room." My mom has an air of bitchiness.

"But you just said you thought I wouldn't come." My voice is sounding desperate.

"Well, I can't help it that you think your brother is so bad that you can't 'suffer through' a week on a lake in a beautiful cabin in the middle of summer." Mom's snooty tone hurts my ears.

"I'm not going, Mom." I am practically crying now, my disappointment so severe.

"Well, good, then you can take care of our house, maybe get in the mail and papers and water the plants and clean the pool." She actually has a grin on her face.

My heart sinks. I am nothing to her.

"Sure, Mom." My emotions go dead.

"And maybe you can care for Lucky, too. They will bring him to our house."

"Ken's dog, too? That's kind of hard." I'm certain she will at least acknowledge this. "I still have to work, and I have my own animals."

"I thought you were crazy about animals... and we do a lot for you, Mary."

*****

The vice grip on my head tightens as I try to pull away from the cutting sadness that the Saint Germaine memory evokes. I spent my birthday week working, running to my house to care for it, running to their house to care for it, walking Lucky, then going back to work, then back to my house for my animals, then back to my parents' house to

stay overnight because of Lucky. By the end of the week I
was exhausted, and my birthday was miserable.

While Ken lounged around on a raft and drank.

This continued for 10 years.

The emotional combat of intensely mourning someone who disappointed me so deeply is again battling in
my mind. I wonder if I ever would have heard the words
I needed from my mom. The greatest loss is that now I
will never find out. I used to say 'It's so hard being his sister', only to be hit back with 'It's harder to be his mother,
Mary'. I don't agree. My brain was formed with him and
was always in the submissive younger sister role. I was
smaller, half his size our whole lives, and being female
didn't help give me power. My parents were adults when
they 'met' him, brains fully formed, bigger than him until
his 20s, and powerful by the backing of the law for 18
years *and* by holding the purse strings to this day. By the
time I figured out something was wrong with him, I was
already enmeshed, learning about the world side by side,
enamored with my older brother who seemed so much
smarter than me. How could my mom never comprehend
the difference?

That pain has not ended with her death in that it
seems as though my dad is now channeling her, despite
any progress we may have made with boundaries earlier
in the year. I don't have any vision of this sick dynamic of
bowing down to Nek ever coming to an end. Especially
since the intervention was a colossal failure. *Unless he were*

to die, I now think on a regular basis. I try not to hope too much, though, because as I've said many times, his pernicious malice drives him on.

He is destined to outlive us all.

CHAPTER 25

KATIE:

"Let it go, let it goooo!"

I listen to the concert from two little girls in front of me. I recently ended my two part-time jobs, realizing that they weren't a good fit for me. The only issue is that I did not find another full-time role before I did that... which seems to be a pattern this past year. So, I am nannying part-time to make a little cash. It's not much, especially with the deferment on my student loans ending soon, but it is enough to pay my other bills for the time being.

"Can't hold it back anymooooore!"

These two girls are belting at the top of their lungs now and twirling around in their princess dresses. I am playing the role of dutiful audience member, looking amazed at everything they do. Working with kids is something that I have found comes naturally to me. I don't think it is something I want to do for the rest of my life because it is exhausting, but for now it is a great diversion from my life.

"The cold doesn't bother me anyway!"

They finish triumphantly. I stand up from the couch and cheer jubilantly while giving them a round of applause. I am a good pretend audience member. My days as a camp counselor probably helped with that. Kids are the best distraction from any hardships in life. They bring a joy with them that cannot be replicated by any adult. After their concert ends, they collapse quickly into naptime upstairs, leaving me with some peace and quiet for a while. My phone buzzes in my pocket and I pull it out to see Mom calling.

My heart jolts every time I see her name pop up. Since Easter, things just haven't been the same between us. She still goes back and forth about me being the problematic one. I have spent the last few months keeping myself busy and distancing myself from all of it. Mary tells me of the drama with Nek, but I can't let myself get invested in it anymore. However, I have returned to the Milwaukee area a few times since Grandma's memorial and reached out to Mom when I did. I was sick of emotions getting swept aside, so I wanted to take any conversation head on, no matter how intense. I told her that I want to have a relationship with her, but that I'm not strong enough to have one with him. I assured her I would not try to make her leave him if she doesn't want that, but I asked her to respect my need to stay away. She seemed to begrudgingly agree. Mary has been helping me grow and learn which relationships are worth holding on to and which ones are not. I want to have a relationship with my mother, but it doesn't change the uneasiness I feel when I pick up the phone.

"Do you have time to talk?" she asks with a strained voice.

"Sure, how is everything going?" I ask politely.

"Not so good." She pauses.

"Oh, why's that?" I know why.

"Dad has been very angry lately," she tells me.

"What's happened?" I ask patiently.

She lets out a sob that she seems to have been holding back. "He is just always angry, *all* the time. I can't take it anymore."

I knew this would happen. It was just a matter of time. I keep probing her to tell me more.

"No matter what I do, he just yells at me and calls me names. If I'm not making him food, I am cleaning out his hearing aid, or looking for something he lost, or listening to him complain about *everything*. He never leaves me alone. I come home from working both jobs and he always is right there. I just can't escape——"

I sigh as she recounts her tale. One that I've heard from her my entire life. I let her finish everything she needs to say before I begin to speak. She is crying harder than she has in a long time.

"—— I don't know what to do. It's gotten so bad that I actually had the thoughts that if I were to die in the next couple days, I would think 'that would actually be fine by me.' If I don't die from the stress of it first."

"What?" I interrupt. "Mom, that's really serious."

"Well, it is just how I feel."

"Mom, really, you need to get out of there. You can't let yourself crumble because of him."

"I just don't know what to do." She lets out a deep breath. "I'm completely trapped. You were lucky to have gotten away."

My eyes widen in surprise at her words. Is this the same person from a few months ago? My heart softens, and I want to help her. "Well, yes, I suppose, but that doesn't mean you can't be lucky, too. I know that we have discussed this several times this year, but I want to tell you again. We can help you. Grandpa, Mary, and all of their resources can help you get away. They would do it for you, Mom. Just like they have helped me."

"I don't know," she sniffles. "It seems impossible to get away from him."

"It's not impossible, I promise you. It's challenging to break away from what's normal to you, yes. It's like swimming against the current. But you will have help. And it gets so much better."

Her sobs seem to be quieting, so I take that as a sign to continue.

"I know that we have been——" I hesitate, searching for the right wording, "distant this year. But as I have said many times before, I still want a relationship with *you*.

And you can call me when you are stressed about this type of thing."

"I know, Katie," she says softly. "I just hope that this will get better. For all of us."

"Me too—" I pause. "Can you please let us help you?"

"Well, what would you guys do?" she asks, and I can tell she is calming down now.

"I don't know specifically yet, but we can figure something out. You are definitely not alone in all of this."

I can only hope that some of this resonates with her, and we eventually end the conversation. There is still a little bit of time left before I wake up the children, so I call Mary to fill her in.

"Wow," I hear through the receiver as I finish relaying Mom's words. "I can't believe it's gotten that bad."

"I am actually not surprised," I say solemnly, "but is there anything that we can do for her? Like maybe we can go up there and rescue her or something?"

"Well, yes, of course we can do that." Mary's willingness to help is instantaneous. "Do you think that she will respond to it?"

"I don't know, but it's worth a shot. I am not ready to give up on her, too." I realize this as I say it. At times during this year I have hoped for Dad to miraculously emerge—and for Nek to go away, eventually reaching acceptance that he will never be the father I have wanted and craved my entire life. But losing Mom is just too much for me.

Mary said she will talk to Grandpa to make sure he is willing to help. We end our call and I get back to my nanny role, directing my attention to the kids as a way to slow my racing thoughts. Try as I might, the hours tick by painfully slow as my mind keeps wondering about what will happen with Mom… or to Mom.

I check my phone to see a text from Mary:

Mary: Grandpa is in. Can you get your mom to meet us somewhere up there tomorrow?

A small amount of amazement washes over me. Mary and Grandpa seldom leave Libertyville, and for them to be willing to push everything aside and go up to Wisconsin just to be there for my mom purely astounds me. After seeing it a few times this year, I am reminded again that this is what it means to be a family. When you love someone, there are always going to be highs and lows. Despite being mad or hurt, when that person is in desperate need, you drop whatever you are doing and run to them. As fast as you possibly can.

And tomorrow, we run.

———

I listen to the quick pants of Mary's dog, ChaCha, as she hangs her head out the car window, letting the wind hit her face. Mary, Grandpa, and I are all piled into the Camry on the highway to Milwaukee. There is a weird electricity with all of us. It's exciting to actually do something to move forward instead of letting the blanket of hopelessness enclose us like it usually does.

There really wasn't much to it for Grandpa to agree. Mary called him last night like she said she would. He was instantly concerned and agreed to come immediately. Mary cancelled her morning Yoga class that she was teaching, and I am off today. Everything is falling into place.

None of us know how Mom is going to respond to our efforts. She was clearly crying out for help, but I have learned to be cautious when she does that because she is prone to changing her mind very quickly. I texted her last night and asked her to meet us alone. She was reluctant but agreed nonetheless. We decided since Dad is always at the house that we would meet at a neutral place.

This morning, everyone is asking me where to go, so I shoot out the first place that comes to mind. "Georgie Porgies," I say aloud in the car.

"What?"

"What is a Georgie Porgie?"Grandpa and Mary ask at the same time.

"It is a restaurant that is based off a tree fort. I used to go there when I was in high school."

When Mom texts me back her agreement, it's settled.

A short time later, we are in front of the familiar scenery I spent so much time at as a kid. My best friend growing up, Maddie, worked there for the better part of high school so I would usually visit her to get banana splits with another friend. They all knew me by name when I came in, and I got discounts from Maddie as well. A wave of nostalgia washes over me. Back then I never would have thought I would be returning under such sad circumstances.

Mom is already here. She has her typical polite smile when she sees us. We all know why we are here, but she is still in the mode of pretending that everything is 'fine and dandy', as she would say. I go in to hug her first. It feels a little awkward after everything that has happened between us. After I move out of the way, Mary and Grandpa hug her quickly and exchange pleasantries before we enter the 'fort'. The nostalgia hits me again as I look around at the fake tree limbs running through the ceiling and the wooden tables with cards underneath a sheen of glass. This place is meant for being family friendly, and it shows with the parents watching their young kids running around crazily. Happy families. A stark contrast from mine.

We bring our food from the order counter to a table outside that is far enough away to be private. Mom asks us how our drive was and then carries on talking about how nice the weather is today, and then how cool Georgie Porgies is, and I have to rub my temples in impatience that we are talking so surface-like. I do not enjoy small talk with Mom these days when there are clearly more important conversations to be had.

"So, how are you, June?" Mary asks her. "Katie said that you weren't doing so well."

Thank you, Mary, I think to myself. I am nervous to be the voice because I have been shut down in the past. Mom bursts into tears, gushing out long sobs.

"It has been really tense there for a while," she finally chokes out.

We try to coax her to tell us more of what is happening. It's both important for her to be heard for her sake and also for Grandpa, who doesn't always understand the complexity my father brings. She tells us how Dad is always angry or depressed and she cannot escape it. Although she is being sort of honest, I can tell that this is still the sugar-coated version compared to what she said to me just one day before.

"I think you really were lucky to get away from him, Katie," she tells me again as she finishes. I consider her words carefully before responding.

"The thing is, I had a *lot* of people helping me, Mom. I wouldn't be in the position I am today if I didn't have the support of everyone here, and many others. In the world outside of our family, it is clear the way that we were treated our whole lives is not right. And I have found that when asking for help with something like this, people will jump at the chance to do so. And what is amazing is that they will do it for you, too, Mom."

She kind of smiles in response, seemingly touched, but it is always hard to tell with her. Grandpa sits listening intently to all of the conversation and seems to be thinking of something of value to say.

"We can help you, June," Mary adds after I finish. "We can give you a place to stay. I have a new house that has lots of room until you get on your feet again, plus Grandpa has said that we can help with the car since yours seems to be on its last leg. If for whatever reason you need to be closer, we have a friend who has a second house in Lake Geneva that you can stay at and basically go into hiding."

Mary looks at me as she says it, both of us knowing she is talking about *her* house. But it's too soon to disclose that fact, in case Mom doesn't get away.

"But what about careers? I can't just leave my job," Mom protests.

"We are all well connected and will be able to help you with that," I interject again. "But that is ultimately up to you if what you are going through is important enough for you to want to leave your job."

"This is certainly a lot to think about," she responds softly.

"It is, but understand that we will never make you do any of these things. I just know from personal experience that it is good to have options. And we want you to know that you do indeed have that. And that you have people who genuinely care about your well-being."

She cries again. She cries so much that I don't know how to respond most of the time.

"Like I said, it's a lot to think about. I will need to consider my options before I jump into anything." Mom has been fearful of change for as long as I can remember.

"That's totally fine. You ultimately have to do what is right for you. Just know that Katie is right in the sense that we do care about you and want to help you, June. We wouldn't have come all the way up here if we didn't," Mary assures her, and Grandpa nods in agreement.

"Yes, thank you." She sniffles. "It means a lot that you did this."

She may change her mind again and, let's face it, she probably will. But we made a sincere effort to help her and she knows that. The ball is in her court to either accept assistance or let it slide. If there is one thing that I have learned this year, it's that you cannot want to help someone more than they want to help themselves.

I really hope my mom wants to help herself.

CHAPTER 26

MARY:

Ken: I'm sure this is good news for you but I have developed liver cancer. Everybody celebrate.

This is the first contact from Nek in weeks. When his obsessive texting goes dormant you can be assured a storm is brewing. I am never surprised when the next ludicrous storyline pummels our family. I just try to enjoy the respite. But this time his news has actually blindsided me. Surely even he wouldn't stoop so low as to fake cancer when my mom just died from it. He wouldn't do that to my dad, I am certain. A vision of his bloated body and blotchy face pervades my brain. The abuse he has inflicted on himself for decades has to be far beyond what a normal human could take. I am sure his liver has suffered the worst. So much for him outliving us?

I reply: Oh no! That is NOT good news at all. Did you just find out?

Ken: Yes.

Mary: Is there treatment available?

Ken: Please don't take my inheritance. It is for my kids.

Mary: What? Does June know about the cancer?

Ken: Yes but Dad and Sandra do not, and I want to be the one to tell them. Stuart knows. I am worried it will be too much for Dad. This is not necessarily fatal. Will find out more tomorrow. Of course, I can't tell Katie.

Communication stops for the rest of the day, although the situation consumes my thoughts. I think he is telling the truth for once. Can our family take another round of cancer? Heaviness fills my heart, mostly for my dad. I don't think he can survive another major loss.

The texts resume the next day.

Ken: Ok I am now possibly faced with surgery next week. It feels like no one loves me and I no longer wish to be a burden.

Mary: We love you Ken. I know that for a fact. Should I say anything to Katie?

Ken: Someone probably should. She has that right though she appears to hate me so much who knows how she will react if at all. I don't even exist to her anymore. Just tell her I've always loved her no matter what.

I am crying now, but I cannot connect to the emotion. Sadness? Relief? Hope? Maybe he will change? Maybe he will die? Maybe this nightmare will end one way or another? I take a deep breath and call Katie.

"I have bad news, Katie. Your dad has liver cancer."

"Oh geez." Exasperation shoots through the phone. "This again?"

"You don't believe him?" I am frustrated with Katie's coldness for the first time since she moved here.

"I don't," she states bluntly.

"Do you really think he would fake cancer of all things?" I really can't believe this.

"He's done it before, Mary," Katie reminds me.

"But now that Grandma just died from it, do you really think even he would do something like that to Grandpa?" I am incredulous.

"I… do. Yes." Katie is firm.

When our conversation ends, I hang up and crawl into bed, trying to hide from the conflict raging in my brain.

Katie is being harsh.

But isn't that what was always said about me?

He wouldn't do this to us.

But doesn't that sound like my mom talking?

Even he has moral limits.

Or maybe he is just that deranged?

The next day I press for details, simultaneously craving the truth and dreading what I might find out. I still do not want to believe Nek would fake cancer.

Mary: What's the status?

Ken: I just came back from doctor. It is not good. They are going to try to cut it out without killing me. I get the impression from you that you don't give a shit.

Mary: I told you yesterday I was very sad and that I love you. How is that not giving a shit?

Ken: I might get through this. I might surprise everyone.

Mary: How is June handling the news? Maybe I will give her a call.

Ken: Don't talk to my wife about this. She is MY wife.

Mary: When is your surgery?

Ken: Why all the questions?

Mary: I'm concerned. I want to help.

Ken: Next week. Wednesday or Thursday. They will let me know Monday.

Mary: Do you need us there?

Ken: The only person I need there is the one person who won't talk to me.

Mary: Ken, you have all of the rest of us... June, Josh, Sandra, Stuart, Dad, me. Just leave the topic of Katie alone.

Ken: Are you telling me I don't love my daughter? How the fuck would you know what love for a child is? You are so messed up Mary. I can't believe the depth of your selfishness. You don't even want her to see her father when he is dying.

I throw my phone down onto the couch, punching the pillows in frustration. He's doing this to get to Katie. He *is* actually faking it. There are no limits to his madness. Katie is out of his control and in his sociopathic mind he will do *anything* to get her back, to win. My sadness flips to fury instantaneously, and I am now determined to expose his lie. Monday is three days away, the day he said he will get details. I begin to concoct a plan of communication.

———

Monday arrives.

Mary: What is the name of your surgeon?

Ken: They haven't assigned me one yet.

Mary: Haven't assigned one yet and the surgery is this week?

Ken: They haven't given me a date yet either.

Mary: Why is that?

Ken: All of a sudden, I am starting to feel I never should have mentioned this to you. This is the problem, you want to know facts before there are any and I get badgered for answers I do not have.

Mary: I thought you were getting answers today.

Ken: Well for the last time I do not have all the facts yet. I'm not repeating that again. I don't much appreciate it. You are a control nut and this thing is out of your control. Accept that and move on. My phone is going off. I need some peace.

I am getting to him, I can tell. I leave him alone for the rest of the day. He initiates the text thread a few days later.

Ken: Surgery scheduled for next Tuesday. June apparently texted Katie that I was nervous and could use a couple of kind words. Katie's response: No. Just one word: No. I have lost my daughter forever. I watched her birth. I raised her from day one. It just isn't right. Bye.

Mary: What is the name of your surgeon? And what hospital will you be at?

Ken: I can't remember. Some Arab guy.

Mary: And the hospital?

No response . . .

———

Days pass, the weekend passes, and it is now Monday night. None of us have heard from Ken or June in over five days, and the surgery is supposedly tomorrow. I am convinced it is all a lie by now, but my dad is distraught. In fact, he berates me for not believing it. I play along with the lie when my dad asks me to send a text to him.

Mary: How are you? Surgery tomorrow?

Nothing.

Mary to June: Is everything ok up there? My dad is worried. Is Ken having surgery tomorrow?

Nothing.

Tuesday morning, my dad and I are in our usual place at the Cancer Wellness Center where we have been going through grief counseling together. We are a half hour into the session, and my dad has failed to mention Ken. He is talking about the weather and the walls and the air conditioning unit outside the window. Anything but what's difficult to admit in typical Albrecht fashion.

So I dive in. "We think my older brother is having surgery for cancer today."

I can almost hear the brain shift in the therapist's head. "What do you mean 'you think'?"

"He won't share details with us. In fact, we haven't heard from him for several days," my dad pipes in.

"You haven't heard from this person you say never leaves you alone?" The therapist's eyes are wide with disbelief.

I look to my dad to see if her words have impact as to how ludicrous this is, but there is no reaction to be had.

I continue to divulge. "And the last we heard from June, she was having a complete meltdown and wanting to die."

The therapist is clearly upset. "What kind of cancer?"

"Liver," my dad responds.

"Where is he getting treatment?" she presses.

"We don't know," my dad sighs.

"And he said he doesn't want anyone to be with him except Katie." I wink at the therapist from out of my dad's view as I say this.

"Katie wouldn't even call him," my dad scorns. "She is really being awful."

"She doesn't believe him, Dad. I guess he's faked cancer before." I stare firmly into the therapist's eyes as I say this last part.

The therapist's face turns red and heat spews from her mouth. "I am beyond horrified that anyone would ever fake cancer. It's insulting, given what I deal with daily. This is so foul even I am sickened. For Ken to dump on you that he has cancer but not give you details, and for June to say she wants to die and then not respond is downright evil behavior. Unless . . . maybe something *is* terribly wrong?"

I can see the therapist wants to say more but is thinking it through. Silence fills the room until she continues. "There is a thing that police do called a *Wellness Check* when communication has ceased. If you do this, you will either pull him out of his silence or you will find they are not okay."

Not okay? I am wondering what she means by that. Suddenly, murder/suicide images from news stories hammer into my imagination. My eyes widen as I gasp. My dad looks at me with bewilderment. It could be possible. After all, Nek is spiraling downward worse than ever. And it's bizarre to not hear back from June.

Mary to June: Been trying to reach Ken. Last week he had said surgery was scheduled for today. But now no communication. Can you let us know what's happening?

No response.

Another 24 hours passes. I am mostly angry, but a trickle of worry tugs at me.

Mary: June, my dad is very concerned. This is hard on him. He asked me to text you to let us know if you are ok. Last he heard Ken had liver cancer and you were having a meltdown and you felt like you needed to leave Ken. We were at counseling yesterday and they suggested we do a Wellness Check which means the police will knock on your door to see if all is well. I don't think that would go over smoothly for Ken so please just send a text or something before my dad does that.

That got an instant response, like the therapist predicted.

June: We are ok. He has a lot of mixed emotions pent up in him. I'm doing ok now.

Mary: Did he have surgery?

June: No

Mary: Is he having surgery?

June: I have no clue.

Mary: Wow. Are you sure you are ok?

June: I'm ok. He's calmed down now. I'm just trying to keep him quiet.

Mary: Ok. Thanks for connecting. We are here if needed.

Ken: You just texted a threat to my wife to call the police for no reason at all other than we are trying to catch a break from you. You have some serious problems, don't you? I want you to be OK Mary but if you wish to go ahead, we can bring everything you have pulled this year right out into the open. Don't bother my wife again. Stop contacting us for now. Too old for this nonsense. You aren't the only one who knows how to call the police.

Mary: Wow Ken. You said you were confronting liver cancer. We are concerned. Dad is especially disturbed. It's not right to involve us and then just stop communicating. I don't have problems at all. We just want to know what's going on with you. The police thing was just a suggestion from a counselor to do a Wellness Check on you to be sure you are ok. Purely out of care. Why the extreme reaction? Last week you needed our support. We wanted to be there. What the heck?

Ken: Stop it Mary just stop it. Do you ever speak truth anymore? Turning phone off.

Mary: Ok goodnight.

Ken: Goodbye.

Mary: Talk to you soon. I hope.

Ken: Not soon. Don't bother June again.

I refuse to let this go, continuing to poke at him until he's more than uncomfortable.

Mary: Well it was all out of care. So, if that's what you want, then ok.

Ken: You are not being straight here and we both know it. About much of anything all year.

Mary: Not sure what you mean. Last week you said thank you for being there for you. I am concerned about your cancer. What is happening with that? This time a year ago, we faced mom's diagnosis. Dad is struggling with facing it again with you. Why did you just stop communicating after dumping that on him?

Ken: I did not stop communicating with him. Only with you. This is absurd go ahead and call police for no reason. That would be funny.

Mary: But you DID stop communicating with Dad. The police thing was just a Wellness Check to be sure you were ok. Only that. Just since we hadn't heard and you were so sick with the diagnosis. Purely a knock on the door to be sure all is ok.

Ken: Non-stop horseshit! You never quit, and you have used circumstances to drive a wedge between our daughter and us. Are you proud of yourself? Do you lie to others all the time or is it just me?

Mary: Katie makes up her own mind, Ken.

———

A couple weeks later, Katie and I find ourselves hiding in a bedroom at my dad's house with our ears pressed against the door, eavesdropping on a conversation with my dad and Nek. There has been no mention of the cancer since the Wellness Check exchange and neither Katie nor I have heard from him. When the phone rings and we hear my dad say, 'Hi, Ken,' we simultaneously silence ourselves, nodding in the knowing way we now have with each other that the only way to get some truth is for them to not realize we are listening.

"I can't quite hear, Katie," I mouth, and she nods.

Bathroom? Katie mouths and indicates with a point of her finger and a questioning face. We crawl across the hall like spies.

"I still can't hear," I mouth again. "Stuart's room?"

We dart across the hall once more and dive into the closet since that is the wall closest to the phone.

"So you just got home?" my dad inquires.

Pause. We cannot decipher Nek's words—just his morose tone.

"Where's June?" Pause.

"That's very considerate of you." Pause.

"That's excellent news." More inaudible sounds on the other end.

"You sound tired. Why don't you get some sleep and call me tomorrow?"

My dad hangs up and proceeds down the stairs, seemingly unaware of the extra sets of ears.

Katie and I look at each other, not failing to grasp the absurdity that we are sitting on the closet floor together hiding out, another reflection of this family's ridiculousness.

"Excellent news? What do you think that means?" I whisper just in case.

She rolls her eyes. "He probably is miraculously cured from cancer."

We sneak down the stairs, entering the living room where my dad is and give him the impression we just arrived.

"I just heard from your dad." He looks at Katie. His shoulders are slumped forward, his head down in his hands. He looks so very old, at least a decade older since my mom died.

"Oh?" she replies casually.

"He just got home from surgery," my dad continues.

"When did he have it?" Katie plays along.

"Just today." My dad seems shaken.

My head starts screaming because IT'S SUNDAY! Only emergencies happen on Sundays, not scheduled operations.

Katie plays it cool. "Was my mom with him, Grandpa?"

"He didn't want to bother her, so he did it while she was at work. She doesn't even know. Wasn't that considerate of him?"

My dad actually believes what he just said?

Katie looks at me. We exchange another knowing look at the ludicrous nature of this story.

My anger is pounding in my chest, but Katie still manages to stay calm. "How did he get there and back?"

"He took a cab both ways. Oh, and now they say he is cancer free. They got it all and he doesn't even need to get chemotherapy or future scans. Isn't that great news?"

"I don't think that's the case, Grandpa. You can believe him if you want but I…. don't."

"That's pretty horrible, Katie." He is harsh in tone.

Not only can I not keep quiet any longer, I basically explode. "So let me get this straight, Dad. The ever-so-thoughtful Ken snuck off on a Sunday afternoon in a cab, admitted himself to the hospital, had major surgery on his liver, recovered enough to call a cab and came back home all between the hours of 2:00 p.m., when June's shift started, and now, 6:00 p.m.? Without telling anyone? Because he didn't want to be a bother? Since when? And is completely cancer free instantly?"

"That's right, Mary." My dad is condescending with his response. "I think you could be more supportive."

I drop my head into my hands and sigh in defeat. There is no breaking through the denial that Nek's behavior creates in so many who know him. Perhaps they cling to this coping mechanism for sanity because to admit how bad it really is could cause extreme mental distress. He doesn't *have* cancer, he *is* cancer. After all, cancer is an invasive growth that multiplies when fed. It can be treated for a while but often recurs with a vengeance, metastasizing throughout its host and eventually killing it. Nek is just this—an evil condition that spreads destructively and is fueled by the denial of others. The condition is contained at times but comes back stronger, his lethal intentions multiplying and overrunning all truth until we as a family unit are annihilated.

CHAPTER 27

MARY:

Early October is a glorious time of year in the Midwest. The days are bright and colorful, the nights cool and refreshing. Usually, I soak up the season with gusto, but this year I have no joy. Nek has been uncomfortably invasive in my life since my mom passed away. I often wake up drenched in sweat from nightmares and the copious amounts of alcohol I now consume daily to deal with my resurrected past. I get regular texts from him bringing back troublesome memories that I had long ago buried. One text in particular has stuck to my brain and will not let go.

Ken: You've hated me for decades and you are exploiting the situation with Katie to get back at me. I know you blame me for what you did to yourself in high school so don't even try to deny it. You are a very sick person Mary Albrecht. Always have been.

It is amazing how the mind protects itself by pocketing certain events into deep corners. For years, I have seldom thought about that year in high school when the abuse ramped up. Now the recollections handicap me and threaten to consume my very sanity.

*****

I strut through the crowded halls of the main campus high school on the first day of classes. I'm finally in the big building with all the upperclassmen and done with that dingy old building that they stick the freshman in. Now I can really experience high school. I love everything about it—so many people and so much to do. Life just keeps getting better. I am already a cheerleader for my second year, which gives me a popular identity. I love my classes, and my teachers treat me like a real adult. It's going to be a great year.

———

Hopefulness envelopes me as I charge through the front door of my house after school. It's mid-September, I have a date to Homecoming, and he's soooo cute! My heart is fluttering in my throat. So far, being a sophomore is going so well that not even Ken can bring me down.

The moan of a sick animal descends from upstairs. I stop in my tracks, trying to listen better, realizing simultaneously that

Ken isn't in front of the TV. Something feels off, but my parents aren't home. Surely, if I call them, they will say I'm overreacting. 'He's your brother, Mary, why are you so afraid of him?' is the reel that never stops winding in my head.

I creep up each step, avoiding the creaky spots, and follow the unfamiliar sounds to just outside Ken's bedroom. The door is open, and there is a body on the bed. Even lying down, Ken's presence is foreboding. The blinds are closed, and it smells even more putrid than usual. Is that a blanket over his head? The sobs are guttural and frightening. I should run away.

"What's wrong, Kenny?" comes out instead.

"None...of... your... goddamn business!" he snaps and hiccups concurrently.

"Okay." I slink back and meekly turn to escape to my room.

"You are just going to leave me here? How selfish can you be?" He sits up now, face bloated and angry.

"I thought you didn't want to talk to me." I try to remain calm even though all of my senses are screaming.

"I don't!" he says.

"So what do you want me to do?"

"If you have to ask then you really are dumb, Mary."

I feel about an inch tall and am anchored to this spot in fear. My mouth moves to speak but no sound comes out.

"You are so lucky because you have friends, you are popular, you are successful." He is nearly choking through the tears. "I have nothing."

My heart melts like butter in a heat wave. He has never sounded remotely vulnerable. Is it possible he is softening? If I'm the one who makes him sick like my mom says, then maybe I can be the one to fix him? I've always wanted my brother to like me and would do practically anything to make that happen. Yet I'm afraid of him. My trembling body is evidence of his effect on me. I should get out of here until my parents come home. I should not get involved.

"You have me, Kenny. I'll be your friend. Would that help?" spews out involuntarily.

"You would do that for me?" His eyes emit a warmth I've never seen in him.

"Yes, Kenny."

Instantly, my fear morphs into excitement. I'm going to be the best little sister ever! I better even skip Homecoming so he doesn't feel left out. I'm sooooo excited he will let me help him—it's going to be great! I will finally have the older brother I always dreamed of.

For the next couple of months, we walk to school together, study in the library, eat lunch in the cafeteria. After school we play cards, listen to music, play tennis, go jogging. My friends are wondering why I am avoiding them, but I don't care, because I am finally making things better. My parents are thrilled.

*****

Stepping outside on my deck in hopes that the fall air will calm me, I jump when my phone beeps as if it's gunfire. It's him again.

Ken: You were the one who wanted to be my friend first Mary. Don't forget it. You brought everything on yourself. Stop using MY daughter as revenge. Only a sick and twisted person would do that.

He's always had an eerie sixth sense. How does he know that I'm presently in the same memory? I gag with disgust at how much he still permeates my being. Is he right? Did I lead him on? I collapse onto the chaise lounge and close my eyes to the sun, hoping to erase the images from that dreadful era. Instead, the visions magnify as it all comes careening back.

*****

It's the middle of the night and I wake to Ken staring at me from the doorway of my bedroom. He restlessly shifts back and forth, sighing painfully. I pretend to stay asleep, just like I've done all the other times since he started this frightening act. My plan to be his friend is backfiring dreadfully as he has become exponentially obsessed with my attention. He comments on my changing body. 'You are getting boobs.' He grabs my butt as I pass by. He tells me what and what not to wear. 'That shirt is too tight.' He hugs me too long and uncomfortably close.

"I'm afraid of Ken, Mom," I blurt out one November evening once he is in his room. "Can I please have a lock on my bedroom door?"

"I thought you two were closer than ever. Why do you really want the lock? Is it to be with Jeff?"

I knew where this conversation was going and gave up.

———

Another month has passed, and I am not okay. Tears are the norm, not the exception. I fall asleep in the middle of classes. Last week, I ran out of the gymnastics gym instead of working on my routines and never came back. A suspension from several meets is the result. My parents have forced me to see a psychiatrist. Sitting here in the big leather chair at my first appointment, the irony is confounding that I am the one who is here.

After only two meetings with the doctor, he diagnoses depression and puts me on strong prescription drugs. My parents are satisfied because they think pills will solve everything. What started out so hopeful this year is now quite the opposite. My head feels sticky, and I have no idea how to get out of this mess. I don't want to be me, in this role, slowly dying from being with Ken. It was crazy to think I could help him. I should have paid attention to my recurring nightmare. He is just too heavy to pull up.

I look at the buffet of prescription bottles sitting next to me on the end table in my bedroom. Mary Albrecht, take twice a day for depression… Mary Albrecht, take as needed for anxiety… Mary Albrecht, take at bedtime to help sleep…

Clearly, I AM the sick one after all.

It's as if I am watching someone else's hand reach out and scoop up all the bottles. One by one, I methodically open them, pouring the entire contents of each onto the bedspread. The world is spinning in slow motion, my pounding heart the only audible sound, as I resolutely take handfuls of pills and swallow them down until they are completely gone.

Time escapes me. I'm in a fog, every sound is muffled, but oh, I am so happy. This is going to be a wonderful night's rest. Finally, I can get away from him . . .

. . . But why is my mom yelling at me? Can't she see that I'm trying to sleep? I can't even understand what she wants, her

speech is so garbled . . . Is she drunk? . . . Who are these people carrying me outside? Is this an ambulance?

*****

I open my eyes and jump out of the chair, trying to escape from myself. The shame surrounds me like it was just yesterday. My mom was so devastated that I did that to myself but not for the right reasons. She was worried about her reputation. She told the doctors I got my vitamins mixed up with prescriptions. They believed her and pumped my stomach. I was home in a few days, and we never spoke of it again. Even Ken didn't bring it up. Not until Katie came here.

I am disgusted to be me, the person with such a repulsive history. I don't want to go back to that terrifying place where I had no power, no confidence, no voice. Yet it seems as if that very place is chasing me once again, and Katie is the vehicle that Ken is using to mow me down. I am dangerously close to losing control and am fearful that the rest of the sordid secrets will involuntarily tumble from my mouth.

I cannot let that happen.

CHAPTER 28

KATIE:

The holidays are approaching, and I am enveloped in dread. It will be a more intense period of having to leave Grandpa's house and find another place to call home each night. It is always me who has to leave, as opposed to limiting Nek's visits, because they would *never* want to upset him. I've been doing this for over eight months, and I'm fed up. Manipulating my whereabouts to dance around his mania is exhausting. And the holidays are only going to increase the need to dance.

Tonight, I am at Mary and Terry's new house, enjoying a beautiful October evening on their deck after one of Terry's tasty meals. This place feels more like home than anywhere else does now. It's a happy house, and the walls emit warmth and safety. Mary wants me to live here, but we seem to be stuck on how to make that happen without Nek troubling the people I have come to care about, my new-found family. I am so sick of being wedged in the middle, and the guilt is suffocating. I have found a job in Chicago and may be able to move there after I save up a little more money.

Ever since I came to Libertyville, I have had roller-coaster emotions. The deepest part of my gut says that I am doing the right thing. Numerous people tell me this, and it is a reassurance to know that those on the outside are cheering for me. But there is always that nagging one percent of my brain that believes I am the one messing up, as my immediate family continues to hammer into me. I am the one who has the problem and needs to forgive him. The anxiety that permeates my brain never goes away. Forever being the black sheep in the family may be too heavy of a load to carry. I often consider throwing in the towel and speaking to Dad politely like they want me to. But the battle in my head rages at the thought of it. I want him to make some effort to help himself first. I am sick with conflict.

The mood is heavy despite the gorgeous night. The air has a pureness to it that is organic as bright stars twinkle overhead. Terry retreats to the kitchen to his usual spot in front of the TV to smoke his after-dinner cigar. Mary and I remain on the deck, each lost in our own thoughts, relaxed from the wine we are both drinking. We have become so close that conversation is not required for comfort. We get along like a family should, keeping no secrets and always having each other's backs.

Peacefulness alternates with discontent as I am consumed with what to do about these awful holidays coming up. I do not want to be around him. But the guilt of not even seeing him at Christmas will surely be the nail in my coffin. Maybe I can at least pretend for that day? Maybe it wouldn't be so bad to see him. I can pretend that his fake cancer was okay, or that his ordering of illegal drugs was normal. I just want the craziness to stop. In my drunken state, I can feel Mary's gaze on me. Before I have a chance to ask if she is thinking the same thoughts, she speaks.

"Ken raped me, Katie," she says quietly. My head snaps toward her, positive I misunderstood. She has said before that she felt emotionally or mentally raped by him. Clearly, that is what she means.

I look her dead in the eye and see a sadness that usually is not there. "What?"

"He raped me. Ken did."

I take in her blank expression, as if she is immersed in a memory, and I realize just how serious she is. She comes in and out of focus, and the world suddenly goes eerily quiet. My throat closes up, and I cannot find any words.

Mary continues in my silence. "It was a power thing. He wanted control over me, so he took it. He was too strong for me. And there was a lot of anger."

I realize that I should say something to her, but I can't seem to move the horrified expression on my face, my mouth stuck open in shock. The pit in my stomach is growing larger by the second. Is she really saying what I think she is?

"It was disgusting. He would take me from behind. Always from behind."

Something from her words brings me out of my stupor.

"Always? Does that mean it happened more than once?" I keep my feet rooted to the ground although in my mind I am running full speed away from her.

"Yes, though I can't process how many times."

I cringe. "It shouldn't have even been one time."

I truthfully don't want to believe her. I always knew he was fucked up. But this…this was incest. She wasn't mentally raped… she was raped.

"I'm—" I hesitate, trying to formulate what I could possibly say at this point. "—I'm so sorry that happened to you, Mary," I say finally, feeling pathetic with the inadequacy of the words. "Why didn't you tell me sooner?"

She grimaces. "Because it's ugly. He is ugly. And it was long in my past until…"

"…Until I came here." I finish her sentence for her.

"Yes," she whispers, and I can see she is starting to tear up. Monumental guilt threatens to crush me. By *me* staying away from him, I brought him back into *her* world.

Questions. I need to keep asking questions. I don't think I can bear the silence, the entrapment of my spinning thoughts.

"So what about Grandma and Grandpa? Did they know?"

"I tried to tell Grandma. She didn't believe me, of course, figuring there must be something wrong with me.

When it first happened, I had to go to the hospital because I was injured. I told her it was him and got sent to a mental hospital. Inpatient."

"Wait a second… He rapes you and *you* get sent to the mental hospital?" I ask as my mouth falls open in horror for what feels like the millionth time this year.

"I couldn't prove it at the time," she says matter-of-factly. Her eyes look tired, as if she is reciting a hurtful, awful tale.

"Wow," I say as I close my eyes and try to forget the horrible image that keeps surfacing behind my eyelids. I let out an exhale that I feel like I have been holding in for a lifetime. "That is seriously fucked up."

"You're right. It is," Mary says as I see full tears streaming down her face now.

We go quiet again as I try to control the flood of emotions. I should really stay with her and talk this out, but I can feel bile rising to my throat and my hands are losing circulation from being clenched into the tightest of fists. After I realize there is nothing more she wants to say about it, I tell her I need to go home.

Mary walks out with me, looking concerned as I pause at my car. I want to separate from her before she sees how messed up my mind is from this whole thing. From an event that didn't even happen to me. I must be completely selfish for worrying about my own pain and anger about it. I cannot let her see that.

She notices that I am upset. "I love you, sweetie," she says to me as I open my door, and I almost break down on the spot. She didn't deserve him doing that to her. She didn't deserve being put in a mental hospital. She didn't deserve me bringing him around again as he stalked me and then blamed her for all of it. My aunt, who has become my closest friend and confidant, is reliving her tortured past because of me.

What have I done?

"I love you, too," I say sadly with a heaviness in my throat and give her a hug. It lasts for at least ten seconds before I finally pull away. I attempt a small smile, but it comes out as more of a grimace. I don't know what else I can possibly say at this point to make anything better. I am completely helpless. "I'm so sorry again that all of this happened to you."

"I'll be okay. Really." Mary is again reassuring me, not worrying about herself.

I nod my head, unable to speak anymore as I climb into the driver's seat. I give her a small wave as I pull my car out of their long driveway. Holding it together until I am out of eyesight, I turn down a side street with no houses nearby and put my car into park. I am in no shape to actually drive. For such a horrifying thing to happen, I desperately don't want to believe it. But everything just fits. Dad was so fixated on her. He talked obsessively about her secrets and how screwed up she was. He said she didn't care about anyone but herself. He blamed her for his problems and maniacally called her when drunk to say awful things.

She, in turn, was beyond tense when we got together those rare times over the years. She told me she had felt mentally raped by him, a term that I have not once heard before. She talked about how he always wanted control over her. I thought she overreacted to his attempts to hug her and get her alone at the time. She seemed aloof and nervous back then, nothing like the aunt I've come to know. Is this why she always dresses so frumpy? Even her non-exercise clothes are too big for her tiny body. When Nek is present, she is more layered than usual—barely showing any skin even on a hot day.

OH MY GOD.

It all makes sense.

He said she hated him, but he made his disgust for her pronounced and played the victim on top of that. His hatred was never because she was mean to him; it was because he was scared of her. He was scared of what she knew he did. If at any time I felt pity for him and his childhood, it's gone now. Along with the thought of ever putting up with him around the holidays just to make the rest of the family content. None of them know about this, and I cannot be the one to tell them. They will, of course, be even more upset at me, and I will be the villain, but I finally realize that it doesn't matter anymore. None of it does. Not when he has committed the vilest crime a person can commit. Everything that happened to me this year seems so petty compared to what I now know.

Revulsion pounds through me so strongly that my body may implode. The madness of this family runs deeper than I could have ever imagined, and I desperately want to just forget about the whole thing. This is far too much for me—my brain is rattling at the speed of a 100 miles per minute. My fists clench once again as I look around desperately for something to numb myself from the fury scorching me from the inside out. When no relief seems near, I press my now-open palms into the heat of my face and let out a scream so loud, so guttural, that my throat is seared raw and my lungs beg me for air.

CHAPTER 29

MARY:

Katie has found an apartment in the city of Chicago. She is moving away as fast as she arrived, and I can't help thinking it's because I shared about the rapes. As I sit here in the wicker chair at my business, even the sanctuary of the Fitness Loft cannot soothe my emotions. I shouldn't have dumped that on his child. How repulsive for her. Yet selfishly, I feel liberated from the most abhorrent part of my childhood. There is a family member who believes me. This conflict has left me with restless nights since that fateful October dinner, and only nightmares when sleep finally comes. All the humiliation rushes back as I again feel like the troubled one, the dirty one, the one who is scarred. I never wanted to be close again to that very dark time in my life. Yet as I feared, the truth practically forced its way out. The fatigue is making me crazy... this is all too much since my mom became ill. Nek's constant torture texts now invade my brain whether awake or not.

Ken: You have some serious problems Mary Albrecht. You have so many damn secrets most of which I know about. All of them safely stored away though organized and ready for use for your selfish needs when the time comes.

Is he right? Is that what I did when I shocked Katie with the very thing I never wanted to say to her—to anyone? I myself said I feel selfishly liberated.

Ken: Mom told me that all the lies and secrets were something you couldn't help. Are you capable of speaking the full truth Mary?

Is keeping secrets the same as lying? But I tried to tell people. Did I try hard enough?

*****

I'm back in the ER with my mom at my side. I'm bleeding vaginally, am torn and bruised down there, and am in great pain. I'm sobbing incoherently until the doctor gives me a sedative. In my loopy drug-induced state, I blurt out that my brother raped me. Time stops as multiple sets of eyes stare me down.

"You don't mean that, Mary," my mom warns chillingly with her tone.

But I do. I say it again. "He raped me."

"Mary Elizabeth, you take that back right now. I know what you and your boyfriend have been doing, so how dare you blame it on your brother."

"Nooooo," I cry weakly before passing out.

———

There is a nurse tending to me with a gentleness that is comforting when I wake up. "It's okay, sweetie, everything will be fine. We are admitting you to a room so you can rest."

Relief swaddles me knowing help is on its way. I will finally be free of him and be safe.

This gurney has been carrying me for a very long time. The noise level is changing; the halls are getting darker. Where are they taking me? I pass out again, waking up in a solitary room with nothing on the walls, no TV, no phone, no trays, no water, no noise. The nurse at my side pats my hand like I'm senile.

I am in and out of consciousness. Did that really happen? Did my brother rape me? Or was it a horrible nightmare?

But I'm hurt. And it wasn't Jeff. Pounding my palms on each side of my head, I try to loosen the cobwebs.

I made Ken angry . . . I called him a freak, told him that no woman will ever want him...

I shake my head violently to continue remembering.

I was tired from the suicide attempt . . .

I had just gotten home from the hospital...

I am sitting up now as the rest cascades out.

I kicked him when he came after me, trying to hit his private parts. He said I brought it on by threatening to injure him there.

OH. MY. GOD.

I plant my face in my hands, rocking back and forth. I said those terrible words, and he raped me because I deserved it. I really AM the cruel one in the family.

My hospital gown is soaking from sweat as I desperately try to rip it off. I need to get dressed, get out of here, and make it better. Why doesn't this place have a phone? Where is all my stuff?

I will apologize to Ken for kicking him, for insulting him. I will apologize to my mom for shocking her with the ugly truth because I caused it. I threatened his manhood—how could I be so stupid?

Thrashing around in the bed, now tangled up in the sheets as well as my gown, my ears burn from the caustic squealing in

my brain. Stars dance in front of my eyes—and then every-
thing goes black.

*****

Groaning as I stand up, my body is beat up from the memories. I pace around the room until I can move a bit more
freely. Being Sunday with no one else at the Loft, I turn on
some loud music and begin to dance vigorously, desperately hoping rigorous exercise will help me forget. I work
myself into a sweat, trying to cleanse Nek from my body,
but even as I drop exhaustively to the floor, he pushes his
way into my already cluttered brain. He made me dirty,
and high school was never the same when I returned.

*****

I'm back at school for the first time since both hospital stays.
How could I think that no one would know where I was for
six weeks? Very naive to think I could pop back into my life
and pick it right up.

First are the whispers upon entering homeroom. There is a
heaviness in the air as I plop down next to my locker neighbor.

"Hey, Paul," I say cheerfully like I always have in the past. A
cold and distant 'hi' with no eye contact is all that is returned.

Scurrying down the crowded hallway toward first period class, people move out of the way as I pass in the other direction. Are they actually afraid of me?

And then there is the silence; groups of people talking cheerfully until they see me approaching. They stare until they think I'm far enough away to not hear the snickering.

I stop outside my classroom and back against the wall to catch my breath, and that's when I see him. Ken is staring at me from across the hall with a smirk on his face that disgusts me. He must see what he has made me into. He nods knowingly, staring too long with those haunting eyes, then struts off in the other direction.

Dread burns through me as it becomes clear I've been labeled a weirdo from being in a mental hospital. I'm officially an outcast and do not know where to go with this realization. School life used to be an escape from the misery of my home life, being that I was 'popular enough' to feel accepted. Now here I am, the 'messed up one' in both places.

What has my family done to me?

*****

There were more rapes after the first time. Not always, maybe not even a lot compared to some abuse victims. It is bizarre to even think this way—what is 'a lot' when it comes to incest? But the threat permeated my life, and he knew he had complete control over me. I never told anyone again so that I wouldn't have to go back to the mental hospital. I just planned to get away from him somehow.

When he went to college, he came back every weekend. My protests to my parents fell on deaf ears. *'Ken is lonely, Mary. This is his home, too. Why do you hate him so much?'* My mom's repetitive statements still had the ability to confuse me back then.

He dropped out of college after one semester and moved back to Libertyville. Second semester of my junior year of high school through senior year were miserable. I kept the surface going, got good grades, stayed in sports, but I was dead inside. I never found my way back to the 'popular' identity after the mental hospital, and my friends were only surface level at best. I held on until I could go to college.

He followed me to Madison. Again, my protests were ignored. *'Ken wants to go to Madison, too, Mary. We have to give him the same opportunities as you. Why do you hate him so much?'*

I moved to the other side of town, where Ken could not find me, within weeks of college starting. My parents thought I still lived in the apartment we originally chose, but I was not about to live around the corner from the beast. I maxed out credit cards in order to rent another place. Ken was menacing and threatening during the very few times we ran into each other on the massive campus, but I managed to get through the four years there without any more physical rapes.

I graduated from Madison and moved back to Libertyville—surely Ken wouldn't come home now that he was married. But then came that phone call in 1986. And the words from my mom that never go away. *'Ken wants to move back home for a while... God wants us to love him, Mary... just be nice to him so that we can keep the peace'.*

Keep the peace—keep the fucking peace. The mantra of our family literally drove me away.

*****

I wake up peaceful like I have every day during this wonderful summer at my childhood home without him. What to do first? Swim? Read? Go for a...

My stomach lurches as I remember yesterday. He is coming back. It's ALL coming back. I vault out of bed and begin scurrying around my room, stuffing bags with whatever is in front of me. He is not here, yet but I can feel him. He's close... too close. I am dripping with sweat as I run up and down the stairs in a frenzy, loading my car until it needs to expand. I grab food and drinks, jump in the car, and hightail it out of the driveway, glancing one last time at the house in the rear-view mirror.

I am numb as I drive away. Until I'm not.

A tsunami of emotions drowns me as I try to see the road ahead. I'm crazy with guilt, yet giddy with power. I am speeding dangerously but do not care. Every minute is another milestone away from him. I am laughing now, cackling really, but then the sobs return. Is it possible to die from crying too much?

———

It is dusk. I've been driving for a very long time. Where am I? What have I done? Oh my God, I didn't even leave a note. What kind of horrible daughter have I become?

I stop to call home… my mom is very mad. "Please, Mom, please hear me this time. He scares me, I can't live with him again." I choke the words out between gasps.

"He is your BROTHER, Mary—What is wrong with you? What you are doing to me now is far worse than anything he has ever done."

"Mumzie… please understand… I'm completely losing myself, and I am suffocating…"

"Well, go find yourself then," my mom snaps with a tone that cuts me in half. "Just remember that I am his mother, too, and I can't believe you would do something this cruel." She hangs up on me—the woman who NEVER hangs up on him.

I slink down the side of the car and begin to shake with panic. Collapsing into a ball on the ground, I pound my head against the car door, rocking back and forth like a mad person. I should go back. I truly am the cruel one. My lungs tighten. I crawl back into the car and pass out.

———

Prying my eyes open with my fingers, I try to lift my head despite the cement block on it. As I shift in the seat, my entire body throbs. It is morning… did I sleep in my car? I dig around in my bag for a drink. My mouth is sticky and my throat burns. I need a bathroom badly. Where am I?

I fall out of the car, stiff with pain. I take a moment to stretch and breathe before I can register my surroundings. Here in an empty parking lot next to several abandoned buildings, I limp a few steps and turn around several times. There is not a soul present to help me figure out where I am. It is quiet. Too quiet.

I lob back to my car, lock the doors, and peel away to find some life. The lady at the gas station says I am somewhere in Ohio, but I don't remember what town she mentioned. She kindly points me to the nearest hotel and, after checking in, I collapse into a bed that feels more wonderful than anything has in a long time. Did I really just leave Libertyville yesterday? Sleep commands me for the next 24 hours.

It is now day three since I 'ran away' and I am showered, clear-headed, and ready to face the next step. I pause in the hotel parking lot as my car idles. I am literally and figuratively in the driver's seat for once in my life. I'm feeling good about standing up for myself.

This is definitely the right thing... isn't it?

I deserve to save myself... right?

I am NOT selfish, NOT selfish, NOT selfish... I hold my hands over my ears to drown out the guilt that is encroaching on my will.

I should call home.

I should apologize for the way I left.

I should tell them I love them.

I should...

NO, NO, NO!!! They are NOT going to get to me again. I am done being their good little girl. This is MY time. I have to do this. A surge of strength propels me to step on the gas and race in the opposite direction of home. I am sobbing again and choking with anxiety. I can feel him close by, though he is physically removed. He permeates my brain; he is chasing me. I have to get further away.

"DRIVE Mary, GO, GO, GO! Drive away until he no longer haunts you." I am screaming, but no one can hear me. I am gasping for air, but no one cares. I am afraid, but I am free.

*****

I hold my head in my hands to keep it from exploding. Katie's move to the city, her second escape, has shot me back to 1986 with all the old pain searing my veins. I am crying again, which I now do more than not since my mom's funeral. The horrible, suffocating, and decades-long remorse is coming out of every pore.

'You hurt your mother very much,' my dad would say whenever I talked to him.

'How can you do this to me, Mary?' my mom would cry to me on the phone.

'You selfish little bitch. You are seriously fucked up.' Ken would leave scathing messages for months after I left.

The guilt of abandoning the family has oppressed me since I was 22 years old. I haven't admitted that until now.

But here is Katie doing the exact same thing.

Twice.

Time stops.

The tears dry up.

My breathing slows.

My mind becomes sober and lucid.

It all makes sense now.

I'm not only helping Katie. Katie is helping me.

And I didn't hurt the family. The family hurt me.

The lightness of the next moment makes me feel like I'm flying. Suddenly, after all these years, I am able to take a deep breath as if I deserve it. Self-forgiveness washes over me like a warm rain after a storm has passed.

I no longer feel dirty, burdened, ashamed.

I feel accepted, understood, loved.

After a storm, everything smells fresh and clean and the world brightens, sometimes presenting a vibrant rainbow. Birds chirp again, squirrels run around once more, and if you are lucky, a butterfly will come and sit quietly on your shoulder.

There once was a saying I connected with, a saying about chasing ideals and trying to force life to be something else. The message was to let go, take what comes, just listen to the signs. If you do this, you will find that happiness comes and quietly sits on your shoulder like a beautiful butterfly softly making its way to you.

As I sit here now in front of a symbolic rainbow, I'm hit with the realization that Katie and I connected for reasons other than what we were trying to make happen. We took a chance on each other to save ourselves, not Ken, and not the entire family. Because no matter how many friends, therapists, and distant relatives tell you what you feel and do is right, it's not the same as someone who really knows, someone on the inside, someone who has lived through the same storms.

Now, as it becomes painfully obvious that we are not succeeding in helping Ken, vindicating each other is like a butterfly quietly appearing on our shoulders. A beautiful surprise.

A surprise we never knew we always wanted.

CHAPTER 30

MARY:

My dad is shattered. As I sit in the Fitness Loft parking lot, idling in my car, the darkness of the hour parallels the sadness in my dad's voice through the phone. 'Weak inside' were the words he used to describe how he felt after Nek left. It is a cold and calm post-Thanksgiving Day, a day that is often peaceful and quiet. A day that many families relax together, enjoying the relief that the abundant meal is over, hunkering down in their warm homes, grateful for each other's company. But for our family, it's only ugliness. We are separate, distant, guarded, and certainly not thankful.

Broken by Bro, Ken. Again.

Ken and June were at my dad's house today, one day after the actual holiday. I was not invited. Nek erupted as usual. 'Violent' was how my dad portrayed the afternoon. He repeated that word so many times that I had to painfully extract what details I could out of this beaten-down man. Stuart filled in the gaps.

Apparently, when Nek arrived, he stormed into the living room. I envision it clearly as this has been more the rule than the exception for as long as I can remember. No hello, no eye contact, no 'How are you, Dad?' He just stared at the TV and would not engage. June made small talk with them while Ken continued to brood, sighing loudly and scratching all over his greasy body like an animal with fleas, Stuart conveyed. In the typical Albrecht style, they tried to pretend all was normal for a while, that this is fine for a human being to act this way *ever*, much less on a holiday. But shockingly, my dad reached his limit of patience, an occurrence so seldom in my lifetime that Nek's behavior must have been at a level of disgusting beyond imaginable.

"I told them to leave, Mary." My dad's remorse is evident in his inflection. "He didn't want to talk, so I thought he should go back home."

"That's a perfect response, Dad!" I am encouraged by this show of strength.

"But he exploded. He yelled at me for at least 45 minutes. Screamed louder than I've ever heard him do."

On a 'good' day, Nek's voice is menacing and depressed, but when he gets angry the force makes the walls move.

"He was only inches away from my face. And when Stuart tried to intervene, Ken shoved him into the door. Violent...so violent . . . "

My blood boils when I picture Nek's freakishly strong body that close to my dad, spit probably spewing from his mouth, hitting my dad's glasses. He could kill practically anyone with one punch when he is in this frightful state, especially my frail father. And he was physical with Stuart? I try to remain calm.

"We were seconds away from calling the police," my dad admits.

"You should have, Dad," I say firmly.

"He threw his glass of Coke against the wall, tipped over the chair, made a mess…" My dad's voice is now breaking apart. "He just kept screaming, Mary… he wouldn't quit. He yelled at me, '*You are kicking your own son out at Thanksgiving?! What kind of father does that?!*'"

"You don't deserve that kind of treatment, Dad. You and Mom were good parents." I say this out of fear that he will collapse.

"But were we?" I don't recognize this man on the other end of the phone, doubting himself for the first time that I have witnessed him doing, admitting to the barbarity of his firstborn child, his son. Is he actually crying?

I'm not about to tell this torn-up person that 'good' parents would have gotten him help long ago, not giving up even if it took a lifetime. That 'good' parenting would involve boundaries and structure and tough love.

"You didn't do anything wrong today, Dad." This, I feel, is a true statement.

"I hope you are right. We'll see." My dad hangs up.

———

It's three days after the horror show of Thanksgiving week-end. As I enter my dad's house for my usual daily visit, I am confronted with a despondent and remorseful father, slumped over in one of the kitchen chairs with the cordless phone in one hand.

"What's going on, Dad?" I try to sound casual, but the worry seeps out in my tone.

"I just got off the phone with Ken. I apologized for the way I treated him. He forgave me."

"*You* apologized?" The anxiety is instantaneous in my shrill voice. "*He* forgave *you*?"

"Well, I had a part in the argument, Mary." The con-descension is back.

"But you didn't…" I stop right there. It's not worth my energy. "Did he apologize, too?" I ask meekly, already knowing the answer but not wanting to be right.

"No. Why would he, Mary?" my dad spews out angrily.

I walk out of the room in disgust. This family horri-fies me. They don't deserve to be labeled 'family'. The only blood relative I have nearby that has earned this title is Katie. Even though she is only in Chicago, I miss her daily strength, her sane vision of right and wrong for us, and her unconditional support.

That's the only kind of family I want now.

CHAPTER 31

KATIE:

Every year around Christmas, I am poor. I roam up and down the aisles at the dollar store on Christmas Eve day looking for cheap gifts that seem thoughtful. As I look through shelves upon shelves of gawdy photo frames and art supplies, I realize just how stuck I am for ideas. I hate that I am in this situation again.

I love the idea of Christmas. Bells ringing in the songs, people in a giving mode, families happy to be together. There is a magical atmosphere. It is the most wonderful time of the year, after all. And even though holidays in our family aren't ever peaceful, I can't help but feel a bubble of happiness within. A surge of hope that we will be in higher spirits because of the season itself.

I walk down an aisle that has a lot of crazy dress-up stuff. As I run my hand through a pink feathery boa, my mind wanders to the thought of any of my family finding it funny if I bought this for them. It reminds me of camp and all the crazy skits we used to do. I smile at the memory.

And then an idea pops into my head. What if I can give them an experience instead of a gift? It's risky, and they may think it is lame. But it is the best I've got at this point. I grab several mismatched items, pay for them, and make my way to my car.

When I get home, I tell my idea to Sandra and she lights up. We scramble through the house to collect other things that could be of use. It turns out we actually have a lot for this particular game, ranging from lightsabers, Guitar Hero guitars, and hats and scarves of all sorts. We pile everything into a huge box and start writing down the different skits for the game participants.

"I hope they go for this, I think it could be really fun," I say to Sandra as we put all of our writings into a hat.

"I think they will. We might as well try." Sandra is trying to be optimistic. I just worry that Dad will be too angry to join us. We never have a holiday without some sort of blow-up.

———

Christmas Eve dinner comes and goes, and we get to the presents. I look at my box of parcels and hope that my game will *make up for my lack of physical gifts. I timidly get everyone's attention.*

"Hey, I have a game that I used to play at camp. Sandra and I have been preparing it. Would anyone like to join?"

They all pause and look at me. My brother yawns, clearly uninterested.

"Well, what kind of game is it?" he asks.

"It's called Dutch Auction, and it is a very interactive game. Two teams compete against each other to perform a skit that is picked from a hat." They look at me skeptically.

"Well, what kind of things are in the hat?" Mom asks.

"It's something that you will learn to do as you go. There are a whole bunch of different scenarios." I'm still getting no response.

"How long does it take? Annie and I were planning on going home soon." Josh's guard is up.

"Not too long," I half lie.

Everyone looks tired. I'm sensing my idea is a flop.

Suddenly, and surprisingly, they all relinquish with a 'let's just get it over with' attitude. Even Dad.

We team up, boys versus girls, with Dad and Josh on one team, and Mom and Annie on the other. Sandra and I become the self-proclaimed judges. We bring the box of 'goodies' out and dump all of them on the floor.

"Alright, each team can grab some things from this pile. There is no good or bad object to pick but try to distribute the amount between the teams evenly." They look hesitant and tired, being 10:30 at night, but they slowly grab some of the objects and bring them back to their own sides. Sandra and I then take our places as judges in the front.

I take charge of the game. "We, the judges, pick a piece of paper from this hat. There are directions of what you need to do. Some things allow points by being the first to finish, but others are subject to the scores of the judges." Sandra waves with a cheesy grin at this. "So let's begin!"

I reach in the hat and pick out a slip of paper. "Okay, we will start easy. This one is a 'first'. So whichever team accomplishes this task first wins the point." I pause and then ask if they are ready. They wait, staring at me as if wondering what on earth we are going to make them do. I let it drag on for suspense.

"First team to bring something red to the judges," I say. And instantly both teams scramble within their goods to find something red. Josh grabs a scarf and runs it up to us, while Annie simply chucks a red pillow at us. The mood lightens.

Sandra and I look at each other in shock, not expecting this good of a response. As we continue playing, the intensity of each team ramps up. They are enjoying this; I smile to myself.

"Best Fashion Runway. You have 30 seconds to prepare," I say aloud, as they dig through their belongings to present their runway skills. The girls go first, dressed in big sunglasses and crazy hats. I decide to play an old boyband song to set the mood and, as they make their way down our makeshift runway, we all laugh at how much effort they are putting into it.

Then it's the boys' turn. Dad struts down the runway with the pink feather boa around his neck. He begins to shake his hips back and forth as he walks and turns around at the end to jiggle his butt one more time. The whole room erupts with laughter. Dad is uncharacteristically free. He actually looks happy. None of us have seen this in a very long time. It is a breath of fresh air that we all crave.

The game goes on with more stunts like 'creating your own team cheer' to 'best boyband impression', and all of us are crying with laughter the rest of the night. I take a minute to look around at the joy in the room and feel so pleased that I was able to bring this game to them. If someone were to look in the window in this particular moment, they wouldn't think of the horror that has occurred here—they would see a healthy family. For a moment I am filled with hope. While there has been a lot of sadness and anger between us, maybe we will actually be all right.

But deep down I dread the truth that we all know will happen. Our joy will only last in a short burst. Nothing good can stay in this family; it's been proven several times over. This is only a small blip of happiness on a whole radar of despair. As the night and the laughter start to fade, I can't help but feel that blip of time is once again running out.

*****

CHAPTER 32

MARY:

Every Christmas, for decades now, has brought an ominous feeling to my gut, quite the opposite of the bustling joy that many folks feel at this time of year. Songs fill the stores, lights shine on the houses, and people talk with excitement about their plans, their families, their traditions. For me, it's just dread. Dread for not *when* Nek will ruin the holiday, but *how*. It's a given pattern that the more wonderful the event *should* be, the more terrible his behavior *will* be.

The first Christmas without my mom is looming as a day of extreme emptiness and grief for all of us. She was so sick at this time last year that she could not even make it up the stairs to see the Christmas tree. The tree that she would usually decorate with detailed care as a symbol of her reverence for the season. She would look forward to sitting next to it morning, afternoon, and night, preferably visiting with someone she loved. Her final December she had Sylvia do the work, and she didn't want to be carried up the stairs even once to see it. In hindsight, I should have realized that she was close to death for her to not fight for this tradition. She went into the hospital December 27 and died two weeks later.

Now here we are a year later, and I miss her so much I can hardly breathe. This intense pain combined with the usual dread is consuming my entire body. To make matters worse, we are spending Christmas Eve at a Chinese restaurant. As I sit here at this very restaurant, I am disappointed that it is a buffet, so we don't get waited on *and* there is no alcohol served. This is definitely not Christmas to me. But, really, when has it ever been?

Terry and I are hosting Christmas Day for his family tomorrow to share our beautiful new home with them. Our move there, though chaotic in timing, has proven to be a blessing in this painful era. And Terry's family has always been a stark contrast to mine—happy, healthy and fun people, to be sure. There is guaranteed laughter when we get together. We have invited Katie, my dad, and Stuart as well. Katie will fit right in with the positivity. And my dad and Stuart will be distracted by the fun.

I take another sip of the wine I smuggled into the restaurant and try to relax into the moment. It's actually humorous being here on this dark and cold December night. It is an alternate reality to what we've ever done, but perhaps it's a sign that new memories are in order. Nek is 'pouting' from the Thanksgiving fight that *he* caused but still got an apology for. Disgust barges into my thoughts. But at least that means he's not coming down here Christmas Day—at least that's what he says. I shake my head in an attempt to shift my thinking back to the positive side. Either way he will *not* be coming to our new home to stain it with his heinous personality.

Between the heat in the room and the warmth from the alcohol, I begin to feel hopeful. We will start a new tradition for Christmas and replace the pain with excitement. I am determined now to make this happen. Nek will *not* be allowed to ruin one more holiday now that my mom is not here. Things are going to be just fine.

———

Christmas morning, I wake up early to clean. As I do so, I feel my mood lifting more and more. It's a gorgeous home, and I'm looking forward to our first holiday here. It is a lovely day, and Nek is going to Josh's, so what can possibly go wrong?

I have been cleaning upstairs for over an hour when I realize that I left my phone on the charger downstairs, out of range to hear it. Rarely these days am I not tethered to my phone, and a hint of anxiety surfaces. But it is Christmas Day, so who really is going to call? Especially since it's only 8:30 in the morning. I continue cleaning for another 30 minutes before heading down to the main level.

Picking up my phone, my brain flips with what I see. *Missed call, missed call, missed call (3), text, text, voicemail (3)*. I click on one of the texts from Katie, nearly dropping the phone from my now sweaty palms.

Katie: Something's happened and I'm on my way to South Milwaukee. I won't be at your Christmas party. Call me asap.

He's going to ruin another holiday, I think to myself despairingly. He's either in jail or the hospital, I am sure.

I look out onto the deck and see my husband on his phone. He catches my eye and waves me out. "Here she is right now, Stuart." He is sullen as he hands me the phone.

"Did you hear?" Stuart blurts out urgently. Something about his voice is different, and my stomach lurches acid into my throat.

"No, but I can see something is up. What's going on?"

"Ken's dead."

A high-pitched buzzing in my brain clouds the moment. I can only choke out the single word. "What?"

"June found him this morning. He's dead."

My thoughts tumble.

There is no way...

He must be faking...

There is some kind of catch...

He's brain-dead but on life support...

Stuart continues. "She found him on the floor, not breathing. The paramedics tried to revive him before pronouncing him dead. They took him away in a body bag."

My entire body convulses as I drop to my knees on the hard deck floor. It is cold outside, but heat envelopes me as I desperately try to catch my breath. A quagmire of emotions are fighting in my head. The buzzing is now amplified, and I cannot move from this spot.

"Put Dad on the phone," I demand to Stuart. Suddenly, I panic that this news will break my dad, and that, indirectly, Ken will kill him after all. The conversation is a blur, and I can only feel his grief through the foggy words. I am crying now… are they tears of relief? Is it possible to have this much anguish when somebody that you always wanted to go away dies?

As I hang up the phone, I am numb. It is the first Christmas without my mom, I'm hunched over outside on all fours in 30-degree weather without a coat, I have 17 people coming to my house in a few hours, my brother is dead, my dad is not okay, and I'm not sure how to get up.

The bastard won. He gets the Olympic medal for the ultimate holiday spoiler. Broken Nek has shattered Christmas Day from now on. We will forever be strangled by this memory.

CHAPTER 33

KATIE:

It is Christmas Eve. *Great.*

Everything about the holiday this year sucks. I just got done with work and typically would be headed back to South Milwaukee by now. But not today, not this year.

My roommates have already left, so I have the place to myself tonight. I try to convince myself that it's just another regular day of the year, nothing special, no big deal. It's hard to believe that we played Dutch Auction just last Christmas Eve. Probably the happiest we have all been together—ever. I was so proud to have brought so much joy to Dad. It was a diamond that was buried in the dirt for all of us, and the best Christmas gift we could have ever been given. Yet here I am this year, sitting on my couch by myself watching *Elf*, the desire to bring joy to my father the farthest thing from my mind.

My new place is average sized for a Chicago apartment, although my room is roughly the size of a small walk-in closet. I met my roommates online only a week after Mary shared her secret with me, just a couple months ago. I had zero dollars saved up and could barely afford the first month of rent, but somehow I did it. I was not ready financially, but I had to get out of Libertyville.

Our walls are ghostly pale because we cannot afford decorations. My part of the fridge is nearly empty, and my room can fit a twin bed, a dresser, and nothing more. As I listen to the noise of the city outside my window with cars honking and loud music from the neighbors, I know that at least I am safe and far away from the terrifying noise that is my family.

I have not spoken to either of my parents for months. They don't even know where I live, for which I am thankful. After hearing Mary's honesty about who my dad really is, my mind hasn't been able to even flicker towards him without terrible anger pulsing through me. My father is a man of many titles: Dad, Husband, Brother, Son, Coach, and now... Incestual Rapist. I have been working almost non-stop at my very low-paying job here in the city so that I can pay my expenses, but really, so that I don't have to face the truth.

No one at work knows anything is wrong. I don't let that show to the people around me. To them, I am always happy. It's just like with the rest of my life and in Mary's Yoga class. People think they know me, always smiling and optimistic. Little do they realize my glass surface has cracked and is only a moment away from shattering.

I am the spawn of a monster. It sickens me. I try to remember the last time I was happy like the faces surrounding me on a daily basis. Was I ever actually happy? Sometimes I'm convinced it was all a facade to cover the garbage of my life. I think of that pile of junk swept to the side of my childhood room. It seems it will haunt me for the rest of my life, always transforming in to other mounds of figurative junk, melding to the situation surrounding me.

I've heard from Josh that Mom wants my address 'to send me a care package', she claims. If it were just her, I would maybe give it out. However, this year has shown me that anything I disclose with her instantly becomes public record for Nek to consume. A part of me wonders if she and I will ever have a decent relationship again, as I have been so badly burned by her. Josh has also said they want me to get together with them for Christmas. When he mentioned it over the phone a few weeks back, he told me that it's killing them to have their daughter in a big city without an ounce of knowledge as to if she is safe. Which in a normal family, I feel would be acceptable. But knowing what I now know, I don't care.

And while I am still mad at Nek, I can't help but look at my spam messages to see if he has texted me again. It's a twisted cycle of curiosity.

I am still not strong enough to be around him. I wish they would get that. Or at least acknowledge that I am not a terrible person for wanting to be away from that trauma. But they won't do that, and here I am pretending that I am not watching movies alone on Christmas Eve.

Too restless to sleep, I remain on the couch and watch more movies. Sandra calls me around 12:30. She tells me she is homesick since she can't be home on Christmas Eve, even though she will fly in on the 26th. I try to empathize but fall short. She has a different perspective on this family, as does Josh. They see Dad's issues like I do, but they lean towards forgiveness as the way to fix it. I have wanted to forgive Dad in the past, but it never felt right. He is terrible to us and never shows remorse. And the forgiveness of all these years has done nothing to help him get better, get clean. He is killing himself while trying to take the rest of us with him. I'm not going to be part of that destruction. Not anymore.

Something inside of me never trusted the person he is. Now that Mary has revealed the depths of her past abuse by him, a part of me feels vindicated. Even though I have seen the same horrors as my siblings and mother, Mary made me realize that my instinct was right about him all along, that his problems root all the way to his core and forgiveness only goes so far.

No one was there for Mary when she desperately needed help. They told her to 'love him out of it', 'rise above', 'turn the other cheek'. They even said it was her fault, that she made him sick. What is wrong with this family? If Mary and I had been raised as siblings, instead of aunt and niece, I would have fought for her when it was happening. I wish I could have been her ally then.

Sandra interrupts my thoughts when she asks what I'm doing for Christmas Day. I tell her about Mary and Terry's party and immediately brace myself for negative judgement. I have come to expect that from the others with anything involving Mary. She is *always* the one they blame. But I won't do that, not ever.

"Okay, I'm glad you are doing something," Sandra says without real emotion. I can tell she is trying to be supportive, also falling short. We have been distant, different, and tense with each other this past year, no longer knowing how to relate. I cannot handle any more criticism for how I have handled myself since Grandma's funeral, so I change the subject. We hang up just after 1:00 in the morning, now officially Christmas.

I go back to my movie, but as my eyes start to droop and consciousness fades away, I fall asleep in the living room. Several hours later, I wake up stiff and disoriented, bummed that I didn't get into my bed. It's early Christmas morning—I can see the sky starting to lighten.

My phone is on the floor a few feet away, and I see the flashing light on the upper left corner. Groaning as I roll off the couch, I check my notifications and see a few missed calls and texts from both Mom and Josh. No voicemail. It's probably just a guilt trip for not planning to come home today. I hesitantly open one of the messages from Josh, numbing myself from the coldness that will surely be in it.

Josh: Katie call us back as soon as you can.

Weird. He usually has a reason for texting something like that.

Mom: Call me ASAP!!!!!

Despite not talking to Mom for months, something about the amount of exclamation points drives my finger to press 'call' immediately.

"Hello?" she answers, voice strained.

"Hey, what's up," I say with little emotion. We have been so rocky lately.

"Katie, it's about Dad. Are you sitting down?" she says urgently.

"Yes, just tell me what happened," I say impatiently, not wanting to waste time. It's probably him concocting another illness so we have to feel sorry for him.

"Dad—," she inhales sharply, "—died this morning."

As she lets out a sob, I blink once, confused. Mom pauses expectantly, perhaps waiting for my reaction to come out. I also wait, but it doesn't. I don't know what I am supposed to feel. I can't even trust that she is telling the truth. But something about faking death seems a little too much—even for Nek.

"What happened?" I say trying to keep my voice steady.

"He stopped breathing in his sleep. I found him around 1:00 a.m. lying down on the living room floor. I tried shaking him, but he just wouldn't wake up. The paramedics came, worked on him for a while, and pronounced him dead."

I wait for the emotions to come—but there is still nothing. It's as if someone is telling me of the death of one of *their* relatives, not one of mine. I have empathy for Mom, but I don't feel pain of my own about the person who died.

"Oh my God, I am so sorry that you had to go through that," I tell her and mean it. "Are you doing okay?"

"I'm just in shock is all. I never thought that would happen," she responds in a shaky voice.

"I'm sorry I didn't answer, I was just sleeping." I feel the need to explain, guilt taking over.

"I figured, it is still early in the morning," she says understandingly, but I am not satisfied.

"I mean it, Mom. I wasn't ignoring you."

"I know you weren't, Katie." We both pause, the silence between us growing louder in my ears.

"Is there anyone there with you? Josh?" I ask.

"Yes, Josh and Annie are here. They got here right as it... was... happening." She chokes the last three words out.

"I just have to gather some things and I will be there in a few hours, okay, Mom?"

"Okay, well, take your time and make sure you drive safe." Mom sounds robotic now. There is strain in our conversation, but neither of us acknowledges it. We hang up shortly after that.

I am frozen on the couch, trying to process these last few minutes. My father is dead, actually dead. I wait for pain. For tears. Even for relief. For any reaction.

I feel nothing.

I am not ready to hustle up to Wisconsin to see them and their blaming eyes. Typically, a daughter in this situation would rush home as soon as possible. I try to push back the deprecating thoughts of how terrible of a person I am for not doing that.

I shoot Mary a text saying that I won't be able to make it to her party today because something has happened. I contemplate telling her the truth, but somehow I feel that is not my place—especially not over text.

My mind races, so I pace the house to match its speed. Should I pack or take time to mourn? Uneasiness burns through me enough to put my running shoes on and make my way outside. I have never seen a Christmas morning so warm. This is good. Running always helps me sort myself out.

I start my slow trot and feel life breathing back into me. *Everything will be alright. I am tough. I can handle this situation.* I continue my inner monologue for a few blocks.

I halt abruptly when I see a young family in the distance. Mother, father, and daughter going for a walk. I watch how at peace they look. The little girl, no older than three, is running about like toddlers do, and her parents watch her in awe. The way a parent should. Her dad scoops her up and gives her a big kiss on the cheek. They are happy.

My legs buckle under me.

My dad is dead. He is not coming back. Hot tears start to trickle down my face, and I turn back toward my house before the family walks any closer to me.

Stepping onto the porch, I sit on the bench outside the door. Having seen that family, the floodgates now open. My father is gone. I will never have a healthy relationship with him. If I ever thought it would be a relief for him to pass away to give us peace, I couldn't have been more wrong. I don't know how to handle this. My body gives way to several harsh sobs, and I don't even care as other people pass by me. My pain gushes out.

The calm outside is nothing like the storm swirling inside of me. Taking a deep breath and closing my eyes, I try to focus only on the sun hitting my face. For a moment I am somewhere else besides my Chicago neighborhood, where there is no anguish, no confusion, no emptiness, only peace. I begin to calm down.

A buzzing next to my ear interrupts me. My eyes snap open, the buzzing goes away, and then comes back. I don't locate the source until I feel a pinch on my thigh from tiny pincers piercing my skin.

"Get away from me," I exhale as I jump away from the monstrous horse fly biting into my skin. I hate horse flies. What are they doing flying around Chicago in the middle of December anywa—

Oh. My. God. I let out a laugh as the thought occurs to me.

He's back. Dad has already returned.

———

The cabin around me is dimly lit as the train makes its way through the dark countryside of southeastern Wisconsin. The only visible light comes from the individual overheads of other passengers in the cabin, the number of which I can count on one hand. Apparently, most people have reached their families by now and are not taking an hour-long Amtrak late on Christmas evening from Chicago to Milwaukee. In my mind's eye, I picture a family of five, sitting close to the tree with a fire lit in the background. The sweet scent of pine mixes with those of a savory nature that still linger from the dinner earlier. The three children are peeking around the bottom of the tree with a happy curiosity, trying to see what other gifts are available for their small hands to grasp and tear open. The parents give their best attempts at telling the children to wait, so they can learn the act of patience, but they are grinning, too, filled with the joy that the holiday ultimately brings.

I stretch my legs out to change the blood-flow. They just barely brush against the bottom of the seat in front of me from the space that is in between. As I sit in the comfortable seats, I keep waiting for the sadness to sear across me again from the news I was given this morning. But all I think about are images of happy families that are together right now. The idea of my father passing away is dull background music in my mind, similar to what is sometimes heard in an elevator. I think about journaling, but as I pull out my notebook I can't get myself to open it. All the signs are telling me to just be here and now.

My original plan was to drive the hour and a half to Milwaukee. The thought of not having my car as a getaway in case things go sour was a non-option. I was to be there by the afternoon and spend time with Mom and Josh. Sandra will be on a flight late tonight that she booked last minute, despite the fact that she would be arriving tomorrow anyway. It would be ironic if she were to get to Mom before me, all the way from Los Angeles.

The exact moment when I was packed up and ready to face whatever was ahead was also when I realized that my keys had somehow escaped me. Most of the time, I see humor when I can't find my keys—or shoes—or debit card—but today, as the universe laughed at my misfortune, there wasn't an etch of humor in my body after searching for them for two hours. I left my car on the wintery streets of Chicago and am taking the evening train instead.

In the past, being on an Amtrak was associated with only positive memories, from day trips to Chicago to going cross-country to the East Coast. Compared to the light-heartedness of those train rides, never in my life would I have thought that the next one would lead me to the place where my father died 15 hours previously.

I wonder how I look to the other passengers on the train. Do I have this emblem on my chest similar to the scarlet letter? Do I resemble someone who just lost her father? Or someone who barely talked to said father the last year of his life? Do I look as numb on the outside as I feel on the inside? Surely, they are all too preoccupied with their own lives to notice, but I can't help but feel like I am a caged animal, on display for the world to see. As my mind focuses on the background noise again, I see last Christmas Eve replaying in my head. The genuine joy that everyone in the room got when we played that silly, hilarious game. How, if anyone were to see us at that very moment, they would have seen a family that had a normal amount of baggage and no cobwebs hiding in the closet. Only one that was enjoying the moment with laughter that looked to be something of the norm, rather than something they hadn't felt in a very long time. That was one year ago, and the best Christmas of my life. All the stories, all of the memories strung together couldn't come close to capturing the difference a year made for me.

We pull up to the station after endless fragmented thoughts skirt over my vision. I shake out of my stupor and grab my large roller suitcase from the overhead cabinet. A man helps me and tells me 'Merry Christmas' when I thank him. Apparently, the world is still turning, and the Christmas spirit is still out there. If only I could feel it like the strangers beside me. I force a close-lipped grin to the conductor as I walk past, attempting to feel normal in this endless wave of uncertainty.

My fellow passengers greet their people waiting, embracing with voices of excitement. I momentarily don't know where to go, so I stand on the platform and simply listen to the rumble of the train behind me as the cold air bites my face. The last time I was at this train station, we had just arrived from Chicago on our way back from seeing the musical *Wicked.* Dad was supposed to pick us up then. He never showed. It wasn't until after two hours of waiting that we found out he was detained for a DUI and that our van was left in a ditch. A flicker of sadness tingles in my chest as I realize he will now forever not show up. Just like when he was alive.

I know Mom is here; she texted me while I was on the train. I walk down the platform to the winding path leading to an open shelter less than a few yards away. I don't know where I'll find her, only that I will. The darkness envelops me, interrupted by the dim lamps along the path that are placed evenly to guide the passengers. I see a silhouette standing in front of the shelter. I don't have to see the face to know that it is her, the stance and posture of the figure is one that I have known my entire life. She is looking around, not appearing to have seen me yet. I hesitate, not sure if I am ready for this moment. How is she going to react? Will she blame me? I have barely seen her all year, and it has been months without any contact. The last time I saw her, she was threatening suicide, and I was withholding my address. Since Christmas last year, nearly *everything* has changed.

Once I get close enough, the figure turns her head in my direction. I wave timidly to get her attention and finally, she starts to walk down the path towards me. I continue my movement towards her, one foot, then two, working together cautiously in front of each other, like cogs in a slow-moving machine. She is about ten paces away, and I can feel my heart thumping wildly in my chest. What do I say? Do I speak first, or do I let her?

My thoughts are spinning a mile a minute as we get within mere feet of each other.

"Hi," I whisper timidly to her, the silence too unbearable for me to continue with. As we get even closer, I can see tears in her eyes. Her face contorts in pain but, relief washes over me when it doesn't seem to be because of me. Her arms open to wrap me up in a tight embrace. I drop my belongings so that I can hug her back. As soon as our limbs are linked around each other, a deep sob shudders through her back. I feel like I should be crying, too, but for some reason I'm not. I am struggling to feel any emotion, even though I am acutely aware that it's in there somewhere. We stay connected for a long time, as if we are passing silent messages we have tried to convey this past year to each other.

The memories burn through me, invading every inch of my being. I think of leaving the house, how devastated I was to be saying goodbye to Mom. How my heart ached knowing that she wouldn't defend me, but rather stick by him because it was easier. I understood her reasons, but the hurt was definitely there.

I think of how my birthday started out, elated by all the people reaching out to me, showing me their love from all over the world. But then the text from her shattered me completely. While a hundred people were making me feel great, she was the only voice I heard.

I think of the letter I wrote to Dad, begging him to want to get better for us. I think about Mom getting mad at me as I continued to stay away, asking me to at least call him on the phone. I remember reading her what I wrote to him, with tears rolling down my face as I tried to prove to her that I wasn't a bad person.

I think about Easter and all the drama that unraveled from that. I did one of the hardest things I'd done in my life when I told my parents to not come inside the place I was staying. I remember my legs shaking as I tried to look calm. I can see her face vividly as she blamed me for the family's problems.

I think of the terrible secret I have learned about Dad just a couple of months ago. How I could never be the one to tell her now.

I think of how close Mom and I were in the beginning of this year and the landslide downward since then. The endless pain as I wondered if I could ever get strong enough to accept the twisted enabling and see my parents again.

I realize now that there was a small bit of hope remaining deep within that somehow, sometime, somewhere… Dad and I could coexist. That he would see how much I am hurting and do anything to make himself better, and therefore help me as a father should. I won't ever have that chance with him now.

I do, however, have a chance with my remaining parent who stands in front of me. Maybe that is why Dad died on this day... so that she and I could be together on Christmas.

I think of all the relationships that I have built over this year, and how I have grown. Mary's face crosses over my mind. She is no longer just a relative I see once in a while; she is now one of my best friends. I know I will continue to stand up for her whenever she needs it and she will do the same for me. Our bond cannot be broken. Not like how her brother used to do to our family.

Death changes us. It destroys a part of us, forcing us to shed a new skin. Sometimes, devastating events are the only way to create change; an occurrence in our lives that rips us apart until we're nothing but tattered clothes on the ground in desperate need of a tailor to sew us back up again. Mom and I, we hurt each other this past year. We hand-ripped the clothes off each other's backs one stitch at a time. But there is always a tailor out there. We can fix us.

People come out of places you least expect and begin to fix the rips in your spirit. One by one your personage emerges as an actual article of clothing. Intact. Whole. Comforting.

Eventually, the threads become so strong that you even learn how to be your own tailor.

For the first time in a long time, I feel genuine hope that nothing will stop me from doing just that.

28 YEARS AGO

I wake up in blackness, once again confused. The memory of those scary men jolts through my brain, and I thrash around violently to be sure they aren't coming for me. I attempt to lock my car doors, but my hands connect with nothing. I feel the seat beneath me, soft and plush. Is this a blanket covering me? I move my legs carefully to not hit the steering wheel, but again my legs connect with nothing. There is a sliver of light in front of me. Is that the sun?

Reality screams for me as I bolt toward the window and peel back the curtains, revealing a brilliant blue sky and sunshine pouring over the Holiday Inn sign. I feverishly search the hotel room for my belongings, running into the bathroom and splashing cold water on my face. I check myself in the mirror. Did they get to me? I become dizzy with panic. Realizing my breathing is so shallow I'm about to pass out, I force myself to slow it down. Flopping back on the bed, I will my brain to declutter. How I ended up here begins to piece together.

I was lost in the mountains…

I tried to get help at the 'General Store'…

I got away from the scary man coming toward me…

I physically could not drive anymore…

There was a knock on the window… a friendly-looking old lady and her daughter.

"Do you need help, missy?" The lady squawked through the cracked window.

"I… do," I said pathetically.

"Where ya tryin' to be?"

"I… don't know."

"Well, that don't sound right." The old lady looked perplexed.

"I need gas in my car."

"Well, that I got, sweetheart—right here in the back of the pick-up." She showed me a canister.

"Ya don't need ta be afraid… we don't bite."

My hand wound down the window as if it had its own mind.

"Can you help me find a hotel?" I didn't even recognize my shaky voice.

The daughter put gas in my car. They let me follow them until I could see the lights of Roanoke, Virginia, and pointed me to the Holiday Inn. They even told me good luck. I checked in dazed, the clock reading 3:13 a.m., and collapsed into the bed.

Pulling one of the pillows over my face, I now scream until my throat is shredded. I ache with desperation to be someone other than me. I am spinning in limbo with no idea how to land. How will I have a mind without my family telling me what to think, how to feel, what to say? I am nothing inside, merely a shell of a person. What if running away makes it worse? Can I do this?

Can I not?

I think of the future with fearful excitement. I think of the past with bone-chilling terror. I cannot and will not ever let HIM touch me again. Not physically, not emotionally, not mentally.

I AM DONE.

Is this hope I feel?

I peel the pillow off my head and stare at the hotel room ceiling. Inhaling deeply, I hold my breath until it is unbearable. My exhalation is long and cleansing, evaporating all my doubt.

I will do this.

I will start a new life.

I deserve to be free.

I will stay with friends. I will get a job. I will find a voice for myself.

I will NOT go back until I'm strong. I love my family, but they are killing me.

I HAVE to do this, or I will not survive.

———

Maybe someday, someone will understand.